BUDDHISM IN ASIA

BUDDHISM IN ASIA

Traditions and Imageries

Edited by
Suchandana Chatterjee
Anita Sengupta
Susmita Bhattacharya

Maulana Abul Kalam Azad Institute of Asian Studies, Kolkata

SHIPRA

ISBN: 978-81-7541-640-6

First Published in India in 2012

Buddhism in Asia: Traditions and Imageries

SHIPRA PUBLICATIONS
H.O.: LG 18-19, Pankaj Central Market, Patparganj,
I.P. Ext., Delhi-110092, Tel: 91-11-2223 5152, 2223 6152
Br.Off.: 4617/18, Ansari Road, Darya Ganj,
New Delhi-110002, Tel: 6594 6453, 9810522367
E-mail: info@shiprapublications.com
www.shiprapublications.com

Contents

Introduction

Over the years, there has been a revival of interest in the Buddhist tradition in Asia. The spiritual and philosophical content of Buddhism has already acquired a degree of attention in the past. But what sometimes goes unnoticed is the repertoire of images and Buddhist lineages, spread over time and space, personified by scholars and patronized by institutions. Buddhism in Asia is increasingly being projected as a dominant cultural discourse with enormous aesthetic appeal that transcends borders and polities. It is this aspect of Buddhism that the present volume seeks to address.

The Buddhist scholarly tradition is no less attractive, disseminated by monk-scholars who live in the monasteries of Gomang, Sera, Drepung and Gandan and scholar communities of the Gelugpa School in Tibet, Kalmykia, Buryatia, Mongolia. There seems to be diverse trends in Buddhist philosophy and teaching. The features of Southeast Asian Buddhism are not common to Tibetan Buddhism. The experiences of Buddhist communities during times of transition have also varied. The Buddhist communities of Asiatic Russia encountered several challenges in the twentieth century. They faced Stalinist repression in the 1930s with the imposition of Bolshevik "order." The re-ordering that followed was extremely harsh. Since the 1990s, institutions and individuals in Buryatia, Tuva and Kalmykia became actively engaged in the revival of Buddhism and restoration of the Buddhist past. Initiatives of restoration have been undertaken by the Institute of Mongolian, Buddhist and Tibetan Studies (IMBT) and the Museum of the Buryat Scientific Centre in Ulan Ude by collecting photographs, documents concerning the fate of Buddhism in the Russian empire (since the time of Tsar Nicholas II), Russian Mongolia, Soviet Union and the Russian Federation. To formalize a cultural dialogue between institutions of Russia and India on the aspect of Buddhist connections and connectivities, this initiative was concretized on the occasion of the Year of India in Russia in 2009. The Maulana Abul Kalam Azad Institute of Asian Studies, Kolkata has collaborated with the institutes of Ulan Ude to organize a photographic exhibition on the collection mentioned above. The weeklong exhibition *The Northern Reach of Buddhism in Asia-Asiatic Communities Past and Present* (16–22 February 2011) was inaugurated at Kolkata's ICCR centre, i.e. the Rabindranath Tagore Centre on the occasion of the Institute's Eurasia seminar.

The exhibition was followed by a brief address by Professor Marina Baldano, head of historical division at IMBT who described the documentation project that was based on an ethnographic survey of *datsans* and *dugans* that survived the Soviet onslaught or were restored later. The profile of lamaseries and lama scholars and their activities in South Asia and India were also mentioned. After this address, a lecture on "Buddhism in Kalmykia" was delivered by Baatr Kitinov of Moscow's People's Friendship University. These two addresses outline the present volume's thematic about the Buddhist tradition in Asia. Kitinov's essay is about the Kalmyk Buddhists who were displaced from their original homeland in Zhungaria that corresponds to modern day Xinjiang. In his opinion, the penetration of Gelugpa tradition into Kalmyk territory can be traced back to the twelfth and thirteenth centuries when the Oirot khans patronized the lama scholars. But that patronage only survived through scattered links in the sixteenth century in the region west of the Urals. The destruction of the Buddhist institutions and the repression of the lamas during the Soviet period delinked the Kalmyks from their original Buddhist environment centred round Tibetan Buddhism. Since the time of revival of Buddhism in Russia, every step was taken to bring the links between Kalmykia, Buryatia, China and India closer. The role of Buddhism in education was a source of inspiration too.

Tsymzhit Vanchikova discusses the Buddhist monastic landscape in Russian Mongolia and Buryatia. Buddhist ethics revolved round the monastic establishments where the presence of Tibetan monks has been noticed since the time of first contacts when Mongolian chiefs escaped from Mongolia and settled with their Buryat kinsmen in the seventeenth century. Tibetan monks assembled as educationists and missionaries—roles that have been completely erased from memory due to Soviet repression. The Tibetan-Buryat relations have made great strides since *perestroika* not simply due to the spiritual connect but also due to the interactive atmosphere that prevails in the scholarly environments of Drepung, Sera, Dharamsala and Gomang monasteries. Various associations in Buryatiya indicate the substantial links between the Buryats and the Kalmyks and the republican governments' initiative to institutionalize such links. So, Tibetan connections that prevail in Kalmykia and Buryatiya not only revolve round missionary activities but also prosper due to governmental initiatives.

Olga Buraeva's paper strikes a different note. Though it takes into account the foundations of Tibetan Buddhism through Tsarist edict in the seventeenth century, it also points to parallel religious trends. Buraeva therefore, points to a series of alternative discourses about religion, especially those regarding Christian Orthodoxy in Russia. In her opinion, the tussle among religious communities in Russia that has surfaced, especially the confrontations that took place as regional authorities took sides, trying to defend confessional norms of their Russian society, and also sometimes overriding Buddhist sentiments about say, land and nomad property, are seldom considered. The syncretistic ideals have nevertheless been taken up at a later stage, during the time of nationalist revival.

These articles reflect the sentiments of the Eurasian scholars regarding trans-Himalayan Buddhism. A different perspective is implicit in the Indian writings in this volume that make a distinction between myth and reality. Rashmi

Doraiswamy argues that Buddhism was one of the key constituents of the Eurasian imaginary. She illustrates this through an examination of the life and works of Nikolai Roerich, the Russian painter who was inspired by the mysticism of trans-Himalayan Buddhism. She notes that Buddhism and the many legends connected with it created an imagined unitary space within Asia for Roerich that was cultural but not overly political. Roerich created a parallel canon, in which the mountains and the caves signified the utopia of the future world of Shambhala and through this creation transcended the Russian identity paradox of looking East or West, by overcoming the "otherness" of the East and making it a part of his own self. Manju Kak examines the legacy of Roerich in her article. She examines the many ways in which his legacy continues to provoke extensive scholarship, both adulatory and critical. Roerich remains important for Indians since his legacy strengthens the case for India's traditions of composite culture and internationalism. She underlines the fact that in a world that is increasingly becoming fragmented Roerich's work, rooted in the sense of common religious beliefs and shared cultures, assumes increasing significance.

The element of diversity in Buddhist traditions is revealed in other articles. Swapna Bhattacharya (Chakraborti) idealizes the eastern trajectory as symbolized by the pilgrimage tradition in Myanmar. She emphasizes that there exists not only geographical proximity between India and Myanmar, but also a close cultural kinship through an intermingling of various races and religious beliefs, the inner strength of which comes from the regions' age old adherence to Buddhism. In fact she notes, contrary to general perceptions of India-Myanmar relations as having being strained during colonial times, the history of monasteries in Myanmar shows that the people remained in close friendship throughout. In this connection she examines the importance of the Buddhist world of Myanmar for South Asia. She closely examines the linkages that developed not just through the movement of monks but also traders and other travelers throughout history and traces it to connections in the post colonial times. She underlines that promoting pilgrimage or any kind of tourism has become an integral part of India's public diplomacy. This, she identifies as a fruitful act, which has brought an awareness among the common masses about the Buddhist past of India. Similarly, the physical connectivity between Bangladesh and India, through bus service and railways has contributed to strengthening existing Buddhist networks. As India enters a new era in her relation with Myanmar it is important to remember that the foundation of the relationship was made through self-less sacrifice of many great souls, from both the countries who believed in *metta* and true Buddhist values.

The papers in this volume profile Buddhism in South and Central Asian contexts. This volume is the second in the series based on the symposiums organized by the Institute as part of its annual Eurasia seminars.

The editors are grateful to Rita Banerjee for copy-editing this volume.

1
Buddhism in Kalmyk Republic: Traditions and Revitalization

Baatr Kitinov

Before analysing the current situation of Buddhism in Kalmykia, it is necessary to make a historical overview. That is the only way to understand the reasons, why Kalmyks went away from their historical homeland Dzungaria (modern Xinjiang in China), why the Gelugpa School of Tibetan Buddhism is dominant among them and what are the specifics of contemporary regional Buddhism.

Early History

Buddhism first began to penetrate into nomadic Oirat society (Oirats, or Western Mongolians, are the ancestors of Kalmyks) in twelfth and early thirteenth centuries largely due to Uighur preachers. Tibetan Buddhism began to spread among the Oirat people at the time of Genghis Khan's conquests, probably in the form of the teachings of the Kagyu School of Tibetan Buddhism. The Oirat tribal unit and conditions for the formation of the union, which consisted of four main Oirat tribes; close relations among these nomadic tribes who inhabited Dzungaria and Qinghai (Northern Tibet) and Tibetan tribes resulted in the spread of influence of Gelugpa teaching of Tibetan Buddhism and the establishment of this school as the dominant one among western Mongolians. Later, due to the vigorous activity of lamas from Mongolia (i.e. East Mongolians), the Gelugpa teachings began to spread among the Buryats and Tuvinians.

Buddhism had to adapt itself to the existing social structure of the western Mongolians. Therefore, talking about Buddhism among Oirats, it is important to remember the impact of the tribal nomadic structure on the religion's institutions. The state administrative apparatus of Oirats proved to be closely bonded with the tribal social structure, and this matter has been reflected on the organization of Buddhist Sangha among them. As the Russian historian S. Kozin pointed out, "the development of the Oirat feudal system was not founded on the ruins of the defeated and destroyed tribal associations, like in Eastern Mongolia, but by growing into them... The strength of the tribal system among Oirats dramatically highlighted by the tribal system that existed among the Volga Kalmyks until the October Revolution"[1] in 1917.

The position of the lamas in the Oirat society depended on the khans' support and patronage. Buddhism, in its turn, was convenient for the secular power due to religion's idea of unity, because it was extremely important for the existence of Oirat Union. Therefore, it can be argued that the preachers of

Buddhism, being among the Oirats, sought to enlist the support of the khans, and facilitated the establishment of a centralized state. That state (Dzungar Khanate) was established in the middle of the seventeenth century. At that time Buddhism was well accepted as state-sponsored ideology that spread not only among the Oirat nobility, but among the ordinary nomads as well. This universal feature of Buddhism helped it in the early stages of its development in India, where Buddhists were "the potential ally of the ancient Indian states that fought against tribal fragmentation."[2]

The Oirats, adopting Buddhism as an ideology, sought to avoid the appearance of influential religious people in their environment, who would be able to claim a dominant position in the established hierarchy of power. The absence of "reincarnated people" among Oirats and Kalmyks is a feature of highly religious yet secular societies, in which Buddhism was not the all pervasive religion but an ideology of a strong secular state. Indeed, among the Kalmyks, almost till the end of the twentieth century there was no one "incarnated" high-ranking lama (except for Xinjiang Kalmyks).

The Kalmyk khans not only patronized a leading lama of the Sangha (Shazhin lama), but also recognized the spiritual supremacy of the Dalai Lama. It is important to remember that the Dalai Lamas became the secular and spiritual leaders of Tibet since 1642, when Ngawang Lobsan Gyatso, the Great Fifth Dalai Lama, headed Tibet due to the support of Gushi, the Khoshout Oirat Khan. Since then the Dalai Lama has been revered as the head of Kalmyk Buddhist Sangha.[3]

The complicated situation in Central Asia in the second half of the sixteenth century caused the disintegration of the union of Oirat tribes. Kho-Urluk, the chief khan of Torgout Oirats, decided to leave Dzungaria and went with his people to the north into Russia. The remaining Dzungar and Derbet Oirats created Dzungar Khanate in modern Xinjiang in 1635; Khoshout Oirats, after supporting Dalai Lama, established their Khoshout Khanate in the northern part of Tibet from 1642.

Buddhists in Russia

In 1608 the ambassadors of Kho-Urluk met with Tsar Vasily Shuisky, who allowed Kalmyks to roam in the outskirts of unpopulated steppes of Russia. Therefore, 1609 is the date of adoption of Kalmyks under Russian power.[4] Starting to move from Dzungaria at the end of the sixteenth century, Kalmyks reached Don river in southern Russia in the 1620s; by the late 1630s they came to banks of Volga river. The Kalmyk Khanate, formed in 1640–50s, covered the huge territory from the northern Caucasus to the southern Ural mountains, from the southern parts of Russian state up to the Caspian lowlands. Thus, the migration of Oirats (Kalmyks) to Russia at the end of the sixteenth century means, at the same time, the penetration of Tibetan Buddhism into Russia. The long distance from Kalmyk lands to important Buddhist centres (Tibet) and various religious environments have caused Buddhism to prevail among the Kalmyks.

Since the beginning of the Russian period of Kalmyks, there was a clear dominance of Gelugpa School: the frequent embassies to the Dalai Lama, education of Kalmyk monks in monasteries of Yellow Hats (a Gelugpa custom), bestowing Khan's regalia on behalf of the Dalai Lama, and so on. The title "Khan," received from Tibetan leader, was recognized by nomadic society as a consecration of the right to rule over all Kalmyk tribes. Thus, there was the sacralization of the Khan's power. As the famous Russian sinologist E. Kychanov noted, for the Mongolian peoples Khan was the centre of sacral and political power.[5] The sacralization of power was important for nomads, because Kalmyks lived in a dense Muslim-Christian environment. The Khan's receiving of the special regalia from The Dalai Lama also meant the protection of religion.

In pre-revolutionary Russia, the state sought to take into account the interests and demands of the Buddhist people: the monks were allowed to go to study in Tibet, new *khuruls* (temples) and monasteries were built. Interest of the Romanov family in the development of this fairly small religious community is one of the major reasons for the construction in 1913 of the famous Buddhist temple in St. Petersburg.

Eminent Russian orientalists (Nikolas Roerich, Feodor Tcherbatskoy, E. Uspensky and others), Russian ministers (Foreign Minister Alexander Izvolsky, Interior Minister Peter Stolypin) and the members of royal family have been involved in the construction of this temple. Tsar Nicholas II in early 1909 said, "Buddhists in Russia may feel themselves as under the wing of the mighty eagle."[6] On 10 August 1915, the temple was consecrated in honour of the deity Kalachakra, whose teaching was preserved, according the Buddhist mythology, in legendary country of Shambhala, often associated with Russia.

In Russia, the Kalmyks partly became the Cossacks—the special cavalry units—which composed of the Don, Terek, Ural Cossack irregular armies. Despite the policy of Christianization, majority of Kalmyk Cossacks remained Buddhists. Thus, in the late nineteenth century the Don Kalmyk Cossacks have had 13 *khuruls* (Baldyr, Inovaysky, Batlaevsky, etc.), the Terek Cossacks have had 4 *khuruls*. The same can be said of the Ural and the Orenburg Kalmyks. Usually these Kalmyks obeyed not the lama of the Kalmyk people (i.e. Shazhin Lama), but their regional religious leader, Bagsha Lama.

The Soviet leaders Lenin and Stalin stressed for Russia's future and the importance of contacts with the Buddhist East. In 1923, Stalin commented about the Kalmyks, "The Oriental people, organically connected with China, India, have related language, religion, customs... If we allow to make a small mistake regarding Kalmyks, who are related to Tibet and China, it will respond much worse on our work, than the mistake regards to Ukraine. We are facing the East and we need to direct our efforts primarily on the East..."[7]

During Soviet period, Buddhism, like other religions, suffered significant losses. In 1917 in Kalmykia there were about 30 large and 65 small *khuruls* with more than two thousand lamas and novices (in the Astrakhan region there were respectively about 25 and 40 *khuruls*, with the clergy of

1,600 lamas), but by the end of 1930s there was no one *khurul* or house of worship there. In Buryatiya there were about 47 *datsans* (temples) before the Revolution; in the late 1930s almost all of them were destroyed. Only in 1946 Ivolginsky (in Buryatiya) and Aga (in Aga Buryat district) *datsans* were re-opened. Tuvinians have had up to 20 *hure* (temples), but none remained after the 1930s.

The traditional Buddhist heritage was lost and forgotten, due to the geopolitical, historical and other critical circumstances that arose due to several wars, in which Kalmyks participated along with other Russian armies; uprisings of Stepan Razin and Emelyan Pugachev; Christian-Muslim environment, etc. The main section of Kalmyks undertook the exodus in 1771 back to China because of Empress Catherine's inner anti-nomadic and pro-German policy. The vital losses for regional Buddhist culture happened after the deportation of Kalmyks to Siberia in 1943–56. The repressions on the clergy during 1930s led to the disappearance of the Buddhist Sangha in Kalmykia. Very few lamas, left alive after deportation, prisons and other sufferings, organized religious ceremonies and services surreptitiously. In the Soviet Union Buddhism was officially recognized as the only existing religion in Buryatiya. Kalmyks felt themselves deprived of an important part of their old and glorious history.

The situation changed only in the middle of 1980s during the days of *perestroika* in the USSR. Religion was recognized as an influential force in society's development. In Elista, the Kalmykian capital, the first community of the faithful

Buddhists was registered in 1988. The significant changes in the religiosity of the people happened, when the late Ven. Kushok Bakula Rimpoche, who was the famous Buddhist figure, the supreme lama of Ladakh, a prominent leader of Gelugpa tradition, the Indian Ambassador to Mongolia, visited Kalmykia in 1989. In 1991 His Holiness the XIV Dalai Lama Tenzin Gyatso paid his first visit to Kalmykia.

The Revival of Faith

After the Dalai Lama's lectures and meetings with the people, Buddhist religious communities began to appear throughout the Kalmyk republic. Ten Kalmyk males of different ages were granted monk's vows by the Dalai Lama in September 1992, when His Holiness again visited Kalmykia. In February 1993, 22 Kalmyk boys (7–25 years old) arrived in Dharamsala, in Drepung monastery (in Karnataka), Tibetan Medical Center (Upper Dharamsala, two medics) and Tibetan Children's Village (TCV, McLeod Ganj) for education. In the year of 1991 some new unions of Buddhists were formed: the Association of Buddhists of Kalmykia (ABK), the Buddhist Youth Centre, and so on. In different Buddhist centres the self-taught enthusiasts explained to Buddhist adherents the basics of Buddhist practices and teachings. In 1995 in Kalmykia 15 new religious organizations were established, and half of them were Buddhist. The Buddhist houses of worship and *khuruls* were built in different parts of Kalmykia: in villages of Tsekerta, Arshan-Zel'men, Yashkul, Orgakin, Malye Derbethy and others. Now each district (there are 13 districts in Kalmykia) has at least one *khurul* or house of worship. The first big *khurul*—Syakusun Sume—

was built in 1996; the opening ceremony was attended by more than 30 thousand people.

In the late 1980s the first head of the Sangha in Kalmykia was Tuvan Dorje (V. Tsympilov), the Buriat Lama, who was sent on a mission by the leaders of Central Spiritual Administration of Buddhists of USSR (CSAB). He spent much time working on the education of the first monks, organization of the religious services, etc. In June 1992, during the second conference of ABK, the delegates voted in favour of the new leader among Kalmykian Buddhists; it was Telo Tulku Rinpoche (E. Ombadykov, born in 1972). He got the title of Shazhin Lama of the Kalmyk people. Being born in the USA, at the age of eight he was recognized by the Dalai Lama as the incarnation of Tilopa, the famous Tibetan *yogin* and Buddhist teacher, one of the founders of the Kagyu lineage of Tibetan Buddhism. Telo Tulku was trained at the Faculty of Goman (sGo-mang) of Drepung Monastery ('Bras-spungs dGon-pa), which was reconstructed by Tibetan Government in Exile, in 1960s in Southern India (Karnataka).

Gomang is one of the seven existing faculties in the Drepung lamasery; it played a prominent role in the spread and education of Buddhism among Oirats and Kalmyks. From the earliest times of its existence, the Gelugpa school educated and trained many Kalmyk lamas: Lama Andzhatan in the eighteenth century, Geshe Wangyal in the twentieth century, and others. Besides Gomang, Kalmyk lamas also have studied in other faculties of Drepung, for instance, at the Faculty of Shakur (Shag-skor); the most famous alumnus of this faculty was the well known Shakur Lama, who became the head of

Shag-skor, and later played a prominent role in the political history of the Kalmyk Khanate in the first quarter of the eighteenth century.

In the 1990s and early 2000s the representatives of the Kalmyk *khuruls* were educated in the monasteries of Mongolia and Buryatiya. At present, the future monks are trained usually in Tibetan monasteries, located in India (Himachal Pradesh, Karnataka). In Elista, in the main Kalmykian *khurul*, Tibetan lamas have been working since 1993. Also, there are similar people with sufficient training in some local temples. They were invited from Tibetan monasteries located in India or in Nepal. Maybe, some time later Kalmyk lamas will arrive from Xinjiang (China), as it was promised by Shalva-Gegen, the leader of Xinjiang Kalmyk Buddhists, who visited Kalmykia in the 1990s. In 1994, in Elista in a gathering of an international Buddhist forum the increasing public interest in Buddhism was showcased. Books, written by renowned Kalmyk lamas, were translated into Russian and published.[8] For example, the aforementioned Geshe Wangyal, who studied at Drepung monastery, left Tibet for India after 1959; he went to the US, where he became the first Tibetan lama in America. His students became prominent Buddhist scholars, some of them being Jeffrey Hopkins, Robert Thurman and others.

The political leadership of the Kalmyk republic and Russia were trying to exploit the potential of religion, particularly Buddhism, for certain specifically narrow goals. Thus, the new leadership of Kalmykia, which came to power in 1993, opted for discretionary powers for a special Department of Religious Affairs, which later became integrated with the Ministry of Culture and was finally deleted. In May 1992, during his trip to Siberia, Russian President Boris Yeltsin visited Ivolginsky *datsan* in Buryatiya, and promised to help in the revival of Buddhism. In August 2009, President Dmitry Medvedev visited the same *datsan* and reiterated the importance of Buddhism in Russian ethos.

Currently in Kalmykia, along with the Sangha, newly emergent religious groups of laity demonstrate the active concern in propagandizing Buddhism. Growth of national (ethnic) consciousness has led to a revival of traditional values, including Buddhist, which have led to an endorsement of ethnic values. As in earlier times, the old religious holidays and ceremonies are being observed, for example, the mystery Tsam, Zul holiday (birthday of Tszonkhapa, 1357–1419, the founder of Gelugpa School), Tsagaan Sar (the New Year and spring meeting), etc. Since 1991, Tibetan monks have created more than 15 *mandalas*, dedicated to the deities like Avalokiteshvara, Tara, Manjushri, Amitayus and others.

Buddhist communities partly were created with the direct participation of famous Buddhist preachers, who frequently travelled to Russia. Not only the Dalai Lama, Tubden Ngodub—the State Oracle of Tibet, leaders (Rinpoches) of different schools of Tibetan Buddhism, such as Kagyu, Sakya, Nyingma but also others visited their Russian counterparts. The last visit of the Dalai Lama was in 2004, when he blessed the construction site of the main temple in Kalmykia, "The Golden Abode of Shakyamuni Buddha."

Revitalization: Way to the Future

Currently, all Buddhist communities face severe economic difficulties. Unlike other religious societies, the Buddhist Sangha does not have sufficient resources and support at the state level; the government has not promoted the restoration of the cult objects destroyed during Soviet times. Various religious groups, practicing different faiths have a space in Kalmyk society. The present situation can be described by H. Hans's term as "symbolic religiosity."[9] According to Hans, in many cases there is religious acculturation, which leads to a kind of symbolic ethnicity, and loss of identity, with the general cultural crisis.

Cultural development is largely dependent on the ability of its actors (from individuals to groups) to receive, accept and transmit information, to act in accordance with the steps taken for its further development. Fundamentally important is the necessity to have a mental image of one's society and culture, especially behavioral and mental data, for a correct perception of the measures to revitalize the culture and civilization. Thus, the people, in fact, constantly re-create an image of society: re-establishes a chain of "personality-family-society (nature)-the culture," where mental, social (political) and ecological settings and experiences of every bearer of culture is integrated.

Despite existing problems, it should be admitted that Buddhism became an important factor in daily life for many people, forming morals, traditions, customs and national identity. It affects all spheres of life for all those who are inspired by the life of the Buddha. This leads to an overcoming of stereotypes of Euro-centric mentality, i.e. the perception of Buddhism not as religion, but as part of the world outlook is a clear deviation from such stereotypes.

There are many actors that have revived Buddhism in Kalmykia, beginning from the composition of communities among the laity who are followers of Buddha's teachings up to cooperation-building among India, China and other Buddhist states which are able to provide significant assistance to Russia in maintaining and developing the Russian Buddhist civilization. The role of religion in general and Buddhism in particular has been recognized as the fundamental basis for the education of children. It is treated as a special subject—"The Basics of religious cultures and secular ethics"—for pupils of class (Year) IV and V, a course which was introduced in the middle level schools of 19 Russian regions since April 2010. In the new school textbooks there is explanation of the long tradition of religious cultures as Orthodoxy, Islam, Judaism and Buddhism. Kalmykia is the single Russian Buddhist region (other regions – Buryatiya, Tuva and partly Altai Republic), which participates in the Federal educational experiment, being listed among mentioned nineteen regions.

In March 2010, a delegation of teachers and scholars of the Kalmyk Republic visited Tibetan schools that are established in India under the auspices of His Holiness the Dalai Lama XIV. Visit of the delegation has been associated with introduction of a new subject, "The basics of the Buddhist culture" for which about 51 per cent of the youth showed interest. In March 2011, teachers who gathered in Elista for a conference summed up the results of teaching this subject. It was noted that the new subject plays an important role in the education of children.

Buddhism becomes the important field for cooperation between the Kalmyk Republic and other countries of Indo-Buddhist civilization. Thus, for instance, in September 2007 the week of "Tibetan culture of China" in Moscow and Kalmykia was represented by a Chinese delegation comprising of artists, officials, scientists, and so-called Living Buddhas, such as Dzukan Tubden Khaidub and Tajang Tenzin Geleg. It should be noted that high officials from embassies of China, Vietnam also time to time visit the republic. At the end of February 2011, Kalmykia for the first time was visited by monks from the famous Thai temple named Wat Phra Dharmakaya Temple and by the representatives of the Dharmakaya Fund in Thailand, who familiarized themselves with local Buddhism. It was decided that in spring 2011, a mass religious ceremony would be conducted in Kalmykia for which, in March 2011, fifty representatives of Kalmyk youth went to Thailand for a month long educational trip.

Conclusion

Thus, Kalmyks (Oirats in general) are the only Buddhist nation, which having the experiences of long distance migrations, live in the multi-confessional environment of Caspian region in southern Russia. The local circumstances, accordingly, framed the specifics of the organization of the Sangha, teachings and ceremonial activities of these nomads. Socio-political role of the Buddhist Sangha among Oirats and

Kalmyks was defined by the hierarchy of lamas and their role in state administration, by the influence of Buddhist doctrines on the state ideology.

The reality is that modern Buddhism in Kalmykia is shaped not only by the revival processes, by the widespread emergence of newly established Buddhist communities and temples, but also by concrete activities, which reflect the ideas of Buddhism that are reciprocated by the adherents in society as well as in the leadership. Buddhism has become a real force that is capable of exercising a noticeable influence on the social, spiritual and political life of the republic.

Notes and References

1. Sergey A. Kozin, *Dzhangariada* (Janggariad) (Moscow-Leningrad 1940), 56.
2. Grigory M. Bongard-Levin, *Indiya epokhi Mauryev* (Moscow 1973), 235.
3. For more information see Baatr U. Kitinov, *The Spread of Buddhism Among Western Mongolian Tribes Between the Thirteenth and Eighteenth Centuries. Tibetan Buddhism in the Politics and Ideology of the Oirat Peoples* (Lewiston, New York: Edwin Mellen Press 2010), 169–72.
4. In 2009 the 400th anniversary of Kalmykia's merging with Russia was celebrated.
5. Eugeny I. Kychaniv, *Kochevye gosudarstva ot gunnov do man'chzhurov* (Moscow 1997), 290.
6. Central State Historical Archive (St. Petersburg), Fond 821, List 133, Delo 446, 35.
7. Russian State Archive of Socio-Political History (Moscow), Fond 50, List 1, Delo 42, 185–86.
8. For instance, see Geshe Wangyal, *Dragotsennaya Lestnitsa*,

translated into Russian by Baatr Kitinov (Moscow-Elista 1994). Originally published as *The Jewelled Staircase* (Ithaca, New York: Snow Lion Publications 1986).

9. Herbert J. Hans, "Symbolic Ethnicity and Symbolic Religiosity: Towards a Comparison of Ethnic and Religious Acculturation," *Ethnic and Racial Studies*, no. 17 (1994): 576–92.

2

Nikolai Roerich and the Myth of Shambhala: The Lure of Utopic Imagination[1]

Rashmi Doraiswamy

Buddhism in many ways created the imagery of the continent that was Asia. It did more: it also was one of the key constituents of the Eurasian imagery. The identity dilemma for Russia, whether it belonged to the Asian landmass or the European one, was theorized in many ways. If Peter the Great opened the window for Russia to look West, Pyotr Chadaayev (1794–1856), despite his searing critique of Russians and their lack of any great contribution to the world, insisted that he would not give up this land for any other. Russia was also separated from the western Christian world, because it followed Orthodox Christianity. The Slavophiles, as against the westerners, looked inwards and idealized the communal way of life, the *obschina*, Eurasianism, as formulated by émigré Russians Nikolai Trubetskoi (1890–1938) and Georgii Vernadsky (1887–1973) among others looked East and believed that Russia's link with Asia was not merely geographical. According to Madhavan Palat, "As a variant of civilization theory, it identified a Eurasian civilization distinct from the European, or Romano-German as Trubetskoi termed it; it was highly polyglot and was composed of multiple elements, Orthodox, Islamic and Buddhist; and these elements enjoyed their autonomy in a non-merging unity which called a symphony. As a civilization it was not European; yet it was not Russian nationalist despite the preponderance of Russians or Slavs within it, and despite it embracing virtually the same territory as that of the Russian Empire."[2] Others like Prince Esper Ukhtomky were Asianists (*Vostochniki)*, believing that Russia's future lay with Asia for both the Russians and the Asians disliked materialism and had faith in religious belief and autocracy. David S Van Der Oye points out that "Asianism lost its appeal among policy-makers in St Petersburg after the catastrophic war with Japan.... In emigration the Eurasianists revived many of these beliefs, but with one important difference. Rather than stressing its oriental nature, the Eurasianists argued that their nation was a world unto itself. For the Eurasianists, Russia was neither Asian nor European, but combined elements of both."[3]

The question of identity for Russia has always been unique and distinct, because it is a country that has faced this continental dilemma of whether it must look East or West in order to define itself. This split, in turn, came to signify several other binaries, through the nineteenth and twentieth centuries, with the West standing in for material prosperity and the East for spiritualism. Despite the fact that Central Asia had been the hub of civilizations and the traffic of goods, religions, and scientific and philosophical ideas had gone on unabated for centuries on the Silk Route, the Russian imaginary of the West was synonymous with modernity, progress and scientific development; the East stood for mysticism. If in its relationship to the West, Russia saw itself as lagging behind, in its relationship to the East, it saw itself as the progressive leader.

Roerich and Asia

Nikolai Roerich (1874–1947), painter, archeologist, folklorist, set designer, writer, poet, was an artist who clearly fitted into the Eurasian paradigm, whether he subscribed to it politically or not. Not that he was anti-West; it was just that the East beckoned him more. It also explains why his series of paintings entitled "Banners of the East" have paintings that refer to Christianity, Islam, older religions such as Tengreism (as in *Oirot, Messenger of the White Burkhan* in the Banners of the East series) and of course, Buddhism, among other themes. Nikolai Roerich spent 49 years of his life in the West travelling from Russia to many countries including Finland, Denmark, England, France, Italy, USA. The remaining 24 years of his life he spent in the East, settling down in India, in the North, and travelling to Central Asia, Tibet, China, Mongolia and Japan. Nikolai Roerich undertook two expeditions to Asia. He did not travel to Asia directly from Russia, but from the West to Asia, through northern India. The first was from 1925 to 1928 and the second from 1934 to 1935. Roerich dreamed of setting up a pan-Buddhist federation that would stretch from parts of India and China, across the Himalayas to Tibet, Siberia, Mongolia. Roerich was not a vocal dissident or a political émigré, as were so many Russians during those times. He went through several stance-swings of being pro- and anti-Soviet. He was also looked upon with suspicion for being a spy, though it was it was never clear by and for whom.

His work is usually split into three periods: The Stone Age, The Theatre Period and the Mountain Period. The first is deeply rooted in Slavic culture and the Russian ethos, although there is a harking back to times past that brings him recognition in his country. The second period is marked by his painting for Russian as well as European theatre productions, in which he is gained international exposure. The third period marks his definitive turn to the Eurasian space.

Religious Renaissance

The other intellectual context apart from Eurasianism that Roerich was nurtured by was the Russian religious renaissance that took place from the last quarter of the nineteenth century to the 1920s. This renaissance was not a simple "return" to Orthodox Christianity but a questioning of the institutions of Orthodoxy (in which Lev Tolstoy played an important part), the debating of alternative modes of religiosity (such as hesychastism, in which asceticism and silent prayer leads to individual deification, which influenced Dostoevsky's representation of Father Zossima in *Brothers Karamazov*) and the openness to mysticism, occultism and belief in other religions. Whether it was western traditions of materialist or positivist philosophy or religious traditions, all were in a state of flux at the close of the nineteenth century. According to Ruth Coates, "On the right, the ruling ideology of Orthodoxy, autocracy and nationality, which was revived in a hardened form… after the assassination of Tsar Alexander II in 1881, met the intellectual and spiritual needs of no one... Chief Procurator of the Holy Synod between 1880 and 1905, Pobedonostsev… actively sought to prevent change not only to the Synodal system but also to every other area of Russia's cultural life, notably in the area of freedom of speech."[4]

This religious renaissance occurred side by side with the upswing of the revolutionary movement. There was a sense of collapse and chaos and a distinct premonition of a change in the order of things. The crisis of Orthodox Christianity, of autocracy, the 1905 Revolution, the First World War and the October Revolution imparted a feeling of an apocalyptic meltdown. While some felt the presence of Anti-Christ, others thought that post-apocalypse, there would be a utopian *sobornost*. According to Vsevolod Volodarsky, "The change of centuries, the contradictory nature of cultural processes, in which, on the hand, the phenomena of crisis and fall and on the other, the birth of the new—came together, was often represented by the intelligentsia of the time as the characteristic symptoms of the catastrophic nature of the times... The sharpened perception of time moving on in the cultural field played an important role. There was the feeling of the loss of creative and spiritual ideals, which had come to them from the nineteenth century, the search for new orientations in life and art, the almost diseased experience of two worlds: the life of dreams and the life of prosaicness and emptiness. The response to this was the huge wave of neoromantic distractions, the idealization of the past, especially the national past, the growth of interest in mysticism, theosophy, religious-philosophical problems…and ethics, taking into consideration the eastern spiritual traditions, with a rethinking…of the role of Russia in the evolution of mankind."[5]

Berenice Rosenthal states that "The religious philosophers of the Russian Silver Age were humanists. They foregrounded man's spiritual and psychological needs, raised issues of meaning and values, and exalted human agency and creativity. They wanted to sanctify the world, including 'the flesh'... Their philosophy incorporated aspects of Orthodox Christianity, such as anti-rationalism, the apotheosis of beauty, transfiguration, deification, and a holistic ontology. The last aspiration underlay their desire for 'integral knowledge' in epistemology, 'total unity' (*vseedinstvo*) in metaphysics, and their social ideal—*sobornost'* (a free society united by love and common ideals whose members retain their individuality). By 'individuality 'they meant self-expression and personal development within a community, rather than apart from or against it. Several humanists exalted Sophia (divine wisdom or 'the eternal feminine')."[6]

There were a group of thinkers who wrote about the change of centuries, epochs and orders in the Silver Age that lasted from 1890 to 1917. The artistic movement that dominated this period was that of Symbolism. This was one of the most important modernist movements of the time that had emerged with the crisis of nineteenth century Russian realism. While some felt the presence of Anti-Christ, others thought that post-Apocalypse, there would be a utopian *sobornost*. Merezhkovsky, for instance, believed that Jesus would rule in the world whose only law would be love in the aftermath of apocalypse. One of the counter-images to that of Anti-Christ was of Sophia, the "eternal feminine" whose range of symbolic associations was wider than that of the Virgin Mary. She was Holy Spirit, Holy Mother, primordial creator. For Father Pavel Florensky, she was the fourth person of the Trinity, for Bulgakov she was the restorer of Order after the Fall, for Solovyev, her beauty was the incarnation of the spiritual and erotic poems could be written about her. The theme of the eternal feminine, formulated by Solovyov, and drawn upon by several artists and thinkers of the Silver Age, was embodied in the image of Sophia, the creative principle of god who expressed the divine wisdom of creation and of total unity (*vseedinstvo*, a concept close to Sololvyov). Solovyov not only wrote erotic poems addressed to her, but also considered her important in his eschatology. Rosenthal points out that "He believed that beauty is the incarnation of a spiritual or divine principle in matter, that art is a form of inspired prophecy, and that the lyric poet has a mission: to bring Sophia down from heaven and find forms to suit her essence. His visions of Sophia inspired Bulgakov, Florenskii, Ivanov, Belyi, and Blok."[7] It was Sophia who, in a sense, stood against the other image that so fascinated the thinkers of the Silver Age, that of Anti-Christ. The theme of the eternal feminine, Sophia, is reflected in Roerich's *Queen of the Heavens* and *Mother of the World* canvases.

Roerich and the Silver Age of Russian Culture

This was the milieu that Roerich was intellectually nurtured by. The sense of crisis, chaos and Apocalypse, the hybrid conception of the Apocalypse/Revolution, the evocation of utopia, the new community (*sobornost*), born of religion/spirituality or socialism, the rejection of the West and the embracing of the East were the dominant currents. Solovyev's *Pan mongolism* (1894) and *Short Story About Antichrist* (1899), Bryusov's *The Coming Huns* (1905), Blok's *Scythians* (1918) and *The Twelve* (1918), are some of the important works that reflect the themes of the age. In addition, they also deal with Russia's relationship with the East. According to Judith Kornblatt, "The anxiety permeating the Silver Age centred in large part between the individual and whole, between the ethically autonomous *lichnost'* and the amorphous masses, and thus concerned the very meaning of humanity... The dangers, even evil, of choosing empty individualism over moribund totality (or vice versa) were often expressed in terms of West and East: the West imagined as the rampant egoism in a disintegrating Europe, the East representing undifferentiated oneness... In this prevailing view of a Russia poised between West and East, the Russian people were fated to transfigure western fragmentation and eastern absolutism into a new age of integration."[8]

The trajectory of Roerich's works in many ways reflects the concerns of the Silver Age. His early works reflected the engagement with *sobornost'*, of the community engaged collective activity, best exemplified in *Slavs on the Dneiper*.

This *productive* collective is seen rarely in his later works. It is the lone traveller, pilgrim, messenger, worshipper, seeker, horse-rider we see. Although alone, the traveller is not lonely: such is the power of what he seeks or what he has found, that he treads fearlessly in a daunting mountainous landscape. Typical of this later period is *Sergius the Builder, Laboring With His Own Forces* (1925, Banners of the East). There is no teeming community here; Sergius is cutting wood all alone in a snow covered mountain range with a bear/dog watching him, almost in boredom, from a distance. It is not that there are no group images in the later works. *The Watch on the Mountains* (1925, Banners of the East) or *Whispers of the Desert* (1926, Maitreya series), have groups of people together. They *are* a community, engaged in some activity—whispering about something of import, or waiting and watching out for a messenger or The Awaited One. They do not, however, form a*sobornost'*, or a productive collective. In fact, paintings such as *Lost in Thought* probably point to a curious hybrid (since Roerich was a master symbols that were hybrids) of the hesychastic tradition in Eastern Orthodox thought and eastern religions such as Buddhism that stress silent, solitary prayer, and union with God.

The Lure of Buddhism

Roerich's engagement with Buddhism came from the social and historical context of Eurasianism and the "Look-East" orientation of Silver Age thinking. It was also moulded, however, by the personal experiences of Helena and Nikolai

Roerich, who claimed that they had had "guidance" from mahatmas of the Himalayas of this world, as well as the world beyond in matters of spirituality. In this, the trail had been blazed earlier by the theosophist Madame Blavatskaya (1831–1891), whose Masters Koot Hoomi and Morya had guided her to the world of the occult in the Himalayas. The Roerichs had their own Masters—Maya and Allal Ming. Nikolai Roerich was also familiar with several occult groups in the West.[9]

Living through two world wars, and deeply anguished by them, it is hardly surprising that Roerich was drawn to Buddhism a religion of peace, tolerance and compassion. John McCannon points out that "...Russia's declining fortunes in WWI caused him great mental anguish. His despair was deepened by the German destruction of cultural monuments in Belgium and France. In later year, this would fire him with a lifelong determination to fight for stronger legal measures to protect art treasures during wartime. At the same time it sharpened his sense that WWI was an apocalypse, a cataclysm signaling the end of an age."[10]

Roerich, in his paintings that relate to Buddhist themes, has touched on Shambhala, Maitreya, the Coming One, Rigden Dyapo, the Ruler of Shambhala, the caves, the treasures of the fabled such as the magical tone, Chintamani, the statues of Buddha, figures of the Buddha himself, the pilgrims, messengers and hermits, Gesar Khan. The range of themes is vast. The utopian moment in Buddhism is exemplified in the myth of Shambhala, a myth that held great fascination for Roerich.

Buddhism travelled out from India to Asia and beyond, and it also "returned" to India in the works of the Russian painter Nikolai Roerich. The trajectory of the spread of Buddhism is thus not outwards and beyond a linear projection, but circular, with returns. Nikolai Roerich was part of the cultural elite of Russia and a modernist. He was also an anthropologist and folklorist and had a deep interest in other cultures. One of the problems that engaged him all his life was the great migration of peoples from one place to another. Modernism, like Romanticism, looked towards other cultures, cultures that appeared exotic, or more "complete" and "harmonious" than the ills of modern, urban life. The Eurasian outlook prompted Roerich to look towards Asia and its religions, its landscape. There was a convergence of the modernist outlook, tempered with realism, and an interest in Buddhism, Islam and Christianity in Asia, along with paganism and shamanism. In his travels through China, Mongolia, Tibet, Central Asia and the Asian parts of the Soviet Union, it was the artifacts of various religions that interested Roerich, the anthropologist and folklorist, particularly those of Buddhism. There was also a sense of the world changing irrevocably, a feeling that gave rise to an interest in utopias. Roerich, the believer in occult, was fascinated by Shambhala, but saw this, as an anthropologist, as one of the many cultural variants in the belief in The Coming Era and the Messiah:

> Before speaking of Shambhala proper, let us remember the Messianic ideas that can be found

> among the most varied peoples of Asia and unite them into one great future expectation.
> The yearning of Palestine towards a Messiah is well-known. The anticipation of a great Avatar near the Bridge of the Worlds exists throughout the broad masses. People know of the White Horse and the Fiery Comet-like Sword and the radiant advent of the Great Rider above the skies. The learned rabbis and Kabbalists throughout Palestine, Syria, Persia, and the whole of Iran, relate remarkable things on this subject.
> The Moslems of Persia, Arabia, and Chinese Turkestan sacredly preserve the legend of Muntazar, who will soon lay the foundation of the New Era...
> The most learned Japanese, the great scholars, speak highly of the awaited Avatar, and the learned Brahmins, taking their information from the Vishnu Puranas and the Devi Puranas, quote beautiful lines about the Kalki Avatar coming on a White Horse.[11]

The theme of utopia for Roerich, who looked eastwards with a receptive mind, without any trepidation or arrogance, unlike so many of his contemporaries, was transfigured into the Buddhist paradise of Shambhala. Russian thought and literature have proved to be a fertile ground for a vast range of utopias. These utopias have often been coloured with a sense of urgency, of realizing them in the here and now rather than in some future time. Of the many divergent trends of thought on utopianism in the nineteenth and early twentieth centuries, Roerich's work drew from the traditions of eschatological, cosmic and Eurasian utopias.[12]

Hybridity

In Roerich's work, well-known figures and images from Christianity mingle with images from other religious traditions, creating a rich tapestry of symbols. Lyudmila Korotkina points out how the Virgin Mary image combines with elements from Tibetan legend: "It is interesting to note that one of the versions of the 1924 *Mother of the World* shows the Celestial Tsarina against the background of a cosmic space, surrounded by Buddhist symbols. In the centre of the lower part of the painting there is the 'tree of life' in the form of a cross with sides of equal length. A similar representation of the tree of life is met with in the most ancient monuments of culture. Roerich represented the cross with equal rays, which according to traditions that have come down to us through centuries, signifies the balance between the male and female origins...Down on the right stands a man with a book, on the left—with a magical wand in the hand."[13] The face, with the eyes as the window to the soul, is covered in a way reminiscent of many eastern cultures. There is no sense of interiority to the figure. She is seated ensconced in a stone formation that almost resembles a lotus. This seat is similar to the ones that the Buddha and other protagonists of Buddhist legends are seated on in Buddhist paintings and *thangkas*. The space that surrounds her is cosmic on the one hand, and mountainous on the other, evoked by the jagged rocks and the water body in between with fish in it. The 1924 painting is far more somber: the orbs with rays of light do not light up the surrounding area. The celestial darkness twinkles with stars. In the painting from the '30s, on the other hand, the light from the circular auras fills its surroundings with luminosity. The palette used is one of "cool" colours.

Roerich's deep knowledge of cultures from the East and West gave him the ability to interpret images in completely contrasting ways. The serpent, agent of the devil or epitome of wisdom and regeneration, finds its depiction in paintings such as *The Cry of the Serpent* (1913/1914), *The Doomed City* (1914), *The Serpent of Wisdom* (1924, from the Banner of the East series). For Roerich himself, the mythical images of the past foretold the future. In this they were prophetic. According to him, "In the basic teaching of Buddha one may already find some suggestions about a future attainment of humanity. Under the symbol of an iron serpent encircling the earth and transporting and laboring for humanity, you see the symbols of railways. Under the symbol of flying iron birds, you understand aircrafts."[14]

Roerich's *The Cry of the Serpent* has tall jagged mountains and the rising head of a serpent, crying out with its mouth open, reaching out to the sky. The texture of the snake's skin and the texture of the mountain slopes seem to resemble each other. The mottled surfaces, the oranges and blues used and the rising twisted head of the serpent convey a very deep sense of unease and disquiet. In *The Doomed City* a snake is wound around the walls of the city. Palat points out that "The symbolism and meaning of this renowned canvas could be puzzling and contradictory. The serpent is the Christian metaphor of evil, and hence the city could be trapped in its coils. On the other hand, it may be imagined as the *kundalini*, hence of divine wisdom; and since Roerich had already been delving deep into Hindu and Buddhist religious doctrines for about two decades, he could well have been suggesting that the serpent alone was aware of what the feckless citizens were not."[15]

Symbolism called forth associations that were evoked by the image the artist offered. It was only in the works of some that the associations evoked are ambivalent, evoking contraries. *The Wisdom of the Serpent* depicts an *apsara* land, closer to the heavens than earth, identifiably Indian in the drape of the sari–like dress. In an unusual composition, women in the bottom centre urge a nude woman to rise; two women on the side watch, one of them is holding a *diya*, with her other hand over the flame, the other seems to be playing a flute, while the turbulent sky is filled with snake-like forms. In this floating world, humans are towards the bottom of the composition; the mountains and clouds float in mid-space and fiery snakes like lightning are flying on top. There is a rise in the gaze of the viewer of the composition to the top, in an analogy it seems with the rise of the divine/libidinal energy from the base of the sacrum to the head. There is a closure of the gaze towards the bottom of the frame, and a retreat into darkness. The languor, sensuality, desire, hesitation in a mode reminiscent of Indian miniatures, gives this painting a different flavor.

There is in Roerich a keen eye for hybridity, the cross fertilization of cultures. The paintings on the Chalice of Christ and the Chalice of Buddha are evidence of this. He believed that the Chalice of Buddha was part of the blessed age that was to come. "The Chalice of the Blessed One was brought here from Peshawar and disappeared here (i.e. in Karashahr–RD). As is said, 'The Chalice of Buddha will be found again, when the time of Shambhala will approach'."[16] The belief that Christ did not die, but lived and preached in Kashmir and the mountains of the Himalayas and beyond, has led to the creation of holy places where Christian and Moslem cultures meet: "About six miles of Kasskgar is the Miriam Mazar, the so-called tomb of the Holy Virgin, Mother of Christ. The legend relates that, after the persecution of Jesus in Jerusalem, Miriam fled to Kashgar, where the place of her burial is marked by a mazar, worshipped up till today."[17]

Buddhist Themes

Roerich had heard of Shambhala as early as 1909.[18] The 1933 painting *Path to Shambhala* is reposeful. The glowing mountain of Shambhala is seen in the distance to the right. There is a sense of the unattainable, although the path to Shambhala does not seem to be so strewn with obstacles, and the mountains, too, do not seem to be too daunting, despite the use of the colour black and jagged lines. The characteristic triadic divide of composition with the midspace that is hard to define– are the peaks above the clouds, or some ethereal matter? It is this mi-space that imparts the sense of the distance between us and

Shambhala, characteristically again, conceived as mountain and cave—height and depth. The 1926 monochrome *March of Shambhala* is turbulent, with clouds, animals and men—all caught in a whirl of forward movement, in the heavenly skies. This painting captures the advent Shambhala as an event of conflict, maybe conquest. This is more in keeping with the Mongolian legend of Gesar Khan, who will lead the people to salvation. Gesar Khan is cast in the image of a warrior who fights for the righteous: Roerich says, "The arrow is the sign of Gesar Khan...Gesar Khan is armed with arrows of thunder and the predestined army is soon ready to come out of the sacred land for the salvation of mankind."[19]

Gesar Khan, the hero of Tibetan and Mongolian epics has, in lamaist thought, come to be identified with the last ruler of Northern Shambhala, Rigden Dyapo. Gesar Khan is supposed to lead the people to a future utopia. This utopia is imagined as a retrospective golden age when the nomadic peoples of this region lived well. There is also the sense of a social revolution in the narratives of Gesar Khan, and in the early years of Mongolian communism, the period was seen as the advent of Shambhala. The Roerich Expedition in Mongolia in 1926 and 1927 reported that there were legends, prophesies and ballads about the future war of Shambhala that not only inspired religious movements, but also armies: "It also reported that the Mongol soldiers of Sukhe Bator, who after 1920 established a semi-Soviet regime in Outer Mongolia, and was called by Owen Lattimore a Mongol counterpart of Lenin, composed battle songs about Shambhala that were sung in the Mongol Revolution: 'The song begins with the words *Jang Shambal-in dayin* or *The War of Northern Shambhala* and calls upon the warriors of Mongolia to rise for the Holy War of liberating the country from oppressing enemies. *Let us all die in this war and be reborn as warriors of Shambhal-in Khan* go the song.'"[20]

The 1941 painting of *Gesar Khan*, riding a horse with the sword raised, captures the myth in a rhetorical way with the fiery skies taking up the most space in the composition and the mountains in the lower foreground. The rider has a long road ahead, but he is up to facing the challenge. Roerich returned to the theme of Gesar before he died in 1947 with *The Abode of Gesar*. The rocky, huge and immovable mountain that overwhelms the space of the composition is a metonymic trope for both the Kingdom and its Ruler. If the first painting gives a sense of the mission to be accomplished, the second is about immutability. The Abode of Gesar stares back at the viewer, face-on. Although there is no opening out of space and the sense of expanse as in the 1941 painting, in one of his last works, Roerich seems to have reiterated his belief in the Land of Shambhala. Even though the colours used are soft, there is no "opening" into this abode of the Warrior. There is no hopelessness; yet the mountain is all exteriority, unlike the mountain in Path to Shambhala that though distant, entices you with its "interiority."

Command of Rigden Djapo (1926–27) shows the Ruler of Shambhala giving orders to his men. He is ensconced in a cave at the top of a mountain and his people set out on horses to the lower depths to spread his word. The line of projection in the composition is from up to down and out, imparting a sense of urgency to a command that has to be carried out.

The third figure of the future ruler of the utopian kingdom was Maitreya. This figure, interestingly, is represented as a statue in *Maitreya the Conqueror* (1926). Roerich the painter represents the gigantic statues that are to be found of Maitreya. On the road from Srinagar to Leh are many monasteries, says Roerich: "Maulbeck—now already a declining monastery, to judge by the ruins—must have been a real stronghold, boldly occupying the summit of a rock. Near Maulbeck, on the main road, you are startled by an ancient gigantic image of Maitreya. You feel that not a Tibetan hand, but probably a Hindu, carved this image at the time of Buddhist glory."[21] The figure of Maitreya is gigantic, a fact made obvious by the worshipper, who looks up in wonder not at the statue, but at the skies and at the fortress in silhouette atop the high mountain opposite. Hewn into the side of the mountain, Maitreya looks more imposing than the mountains and the fiery sky. Roerich was fascinated by the impulse provided by Buddhism to create sculptures and architecture at great heights in the mountains. He states: "One must have a sense of beauty and of fearless self-denial to build strongholds on such heights. In many such castles, long subterranean passages, leading to a river, were hewn in rocks, so that a loaded donkey could just manage to pass there. This fairy-tale of subterranean passages...has created many of the best sagas."[22] In *Walled Stronghold* (1925/1926), a large statue of what seems to be Maitreya is embedded in the rocks on a mountain top, along with other architectural structures that are empty. A man, in the lower left corner, gazes out at something. It is the sculpture that seems to be guarding the stronghold.

Caves in the Mountains

Caves are another important Buddhist theme that Roerich touched upon in his works. Apart from being the dwelling of Buddhist hermits, for Roerich they are also the opening into *the interior world* of the mountains. He writes, "Each entrance to a cave suggests that someone has already entered there. Every creek—especially the subterranean creeks—draw one's fantasy to the underground passages. In many places of Central Asia, they speak of the Agharti, the subterranean people. In numerous beautiful legends they outline the same story of how the bet people abandoned the treacherous earth and sought salvation in hidden countries where they acquired new forces and conquered powerful energies."[23] These caves are natural formations in the mountains, opening in rocks, that otherwise look impenetrable as in *Rocks of the Buddhist Caves* (1927/1928). In the *Power of the Caves* (1925/1926), the openings in the side of the mountain resemble the formations of an anthill. The gigantic nature of these openings is slowly revealed as our gaze is drawn into the cave and we see sculptures on the walls and the roofs of the caves.

The cave is the entrance into other subterranean lands. This belief in worlds that exist below or deep inside the earth, has its modernist counterpart in Expressionism. The topography of the netherworld, this world and the world above was a staple of the Expressionist imagination. The forces of the night, of evil, of darkness are granted a space of their own in this aesthetic. In Roerich, who had his own links with the Modernist movement in the West,[24] the underground is a space filled with wonder. While he was as an artist, no doubt aware of the Gothic, Symbolist and Expressionist imaginings of the world under the ground, he made the nether world the object of his attention, but from a different point of view. Shambhala, in some interpretations existed below the known earth. The mystery of the interiors of the mountains, and of the caves, too, fascinated him. For Roerich, the evidence of subterranean worlds was in the unexpected juxtapositions that Nature threw up: "In the foothills of the Himalayas are many caves and it is said from these caves, subterranean passages proceed far below Kanchenjunga. Some have even seen the stone door which has never been opened, because the date has not arrived. The deep passages proceed to the Splendid Valley. You can realize the origin and reality of such legends, when you are acquainted with the unsuspected formations of Himalayan nature, when you perceive how closely together are glaciers and rich vegetation."[25] Roerich also envisioned the existence of Shambhala in the space between the Altai and the Himalayas. Osterrrieder points out that "The Altai Mountains— and more widely Siberia—were at the very core of the Great Plan, an indispensable component of the 'New Country', because Roerich believed that Altai would become a double for Shambhala— as the fabled land of *Belovodye*, or the Land of White Waters, celebrated in numerous Russian folk legends... Drawing upon the tales of the underground Agartha...Roerich envisioned an intricate network of tunnels and chambers linking the Altai with the Himalayas."[26]

The painting *Buddha, the Conqueror* (1925) can only be understood if one has this fascination that Roerich had for the underground in mind. Buddha is reposeful and resplendent. The surroundings he is in, is however, have jagged forms like stalactites jutting out from the roof of the caves. The serene Buddha is ensconced in sharply jutting mountain-like and cave-like forms, in front of a pool of still water. These surroundings would evoke a sense of disquiet if the cave and mountain were not seen as wondrous spaces full of mystery and the promise of a utopian land.

According to Palat, the cave and the mountain imagery in Roerich went beyond the uterine and phallic associations: "... the female principle was more spiritual, intuitive, and nearer to God; and it complemented male rationality which was inadequate by itself. But the cavern and the mountain yielded perhaps the most important of all symbols, that of the axis mundi. The world we inhabit could be conceived as positioned anywhere along the line from the deepest cavern to the most exalted mountain peak, and no place could be outside of it. As such it was the very axis in which the world turned. .... Mysteries were hidden deep in the underground, in the network of caverns that criss-crossed the earth; from there they rose into the light above, the mountain tops, and eventually to his new world, Shambhala."[27]

The Kyrgyz writer, Chingiz Aitmatov tried to dabble in world literature and global issues after the fall of the Soviet Union. His last novel before his death was a "return" to Kyrgyzstan, literally and metaphorically. He took up issues that bothered his land, but he also created the image of the white leopard that roamed the high mountains in loneliness. Roerich, many decades earlier turned to the mountains, as that height from which he could transcend the problems of everyday life and politics. In order to enter the caverns and the splendorous world they would lead to, one had to first ascend the mountains. This subterranean world was not accessible from the plains. The ascent was necessary before the descent. The mountains in Roerich became the Wall. Beyond the ranges (composed usually according to the triadic principles, in a horizontal or vertical axis, one range would become the ultimate end, the Wall, beyond which nothing could be seen. No valley could be peeped upon, no river flowing beyond the mountains. This compositional principle witnessed in his Mountain Period did not exist in his earlier works. The 1910 painting *Idols (Pagan Russia)* shows an entire landscape, replete with river, hills and clouds, beyond the architectural-sculptural forms. This kind of opening out onto a life of the plains beyond height is rarely encountered in his later work. *Abode of Gesar Khan*, painted in the last year of his life is emblematic: the immutable mountain floating above the clouds, as it were, is the Ultimate Reality. There is no Beyond. The paintings of the mountains and caves and the utopic vision of Shambhala in Roerich are what the French thinkers Deleuze and Guattari in another context called 'a passage from the finite to the infinite, but also from territory to deterritorialization.

Roerich was a modernist. He, however, occupies a distinct place in the movements of modernism of the twentieth century. If modernism engaged with the category of space-time, and critiqued realist modes of representation and created its own registers of the exotic, thus linking itself with Romanticism, then Roerich's canvases of his third period sit uneasily in them. Not for him the fragmentation and breaking up of space in order to incorporate a sense of time as in Cubism. Not even the engagement with line and form in abstraction as in Malevich or Klee. Not also for him the dream-space of surrealism with its simultaneity of past/present/future coloured with memory and desire as, for instance, in the works of Salvador Dali. Nor was it the carnivalesque mytho-social world of Chagall. Roerich returns, through his modernism, to a transformed realism. This is no longer a realism of socio-historical detail, or of the subalterns or marginals as had been made canonical by XIX century Russian realism. This was a realism of representation, but one that was a-social, a-territorial and a-historical.

In the canvases with Buddhist themes, the preoccupation with past that was represented in the first two phases, gets transformed into an utopian future. The Russian, Slavic, European coordinates of his painting at the formal and thematic levels are doubly de-territorialized: not only do they lose their European moorings, they also move from culture into nature. This gets re-territorialized in the canvases with Buddhist themes onto caves, mammoth statues and legendary figures. The passage to the mountains, viewed from a perspective of height that is of the mountains themselves. This is not an aerial view just as it is not a view from the plains. The mountains are viewed head-on. Roerich's utopic imagination thus creates an Asia of height, depth and expanse that is of the natural world that subsumes cultural signifiers. The spatial proportions are such that the human figure is miniscule in comparison and the cultural signifiers along with nature enter the register of what Bakhtin calls “the big time” (*bol'shoe vremya*). Thus Roerich, although he was deeply linked to the Russian Silver Age and European modernist movements, created a parallel register of modernism. The urbanist bias of the movement was ignored and nature occupied the central place; the utopian impulse was largely shorn of fear and dystopia, characteristic of many modernist utopian imaginings; the subterranean world is liberated from the gothic-expressionist representation of the dark underside of human nature and the category of space-time, caught in its complex unfolding in modernist works, is pushed into the realm of the immutable and of “big time.”

The Geopolitics of Shambhala

Roerich’s relations with British, American, Soviet, Nazi, Japanese government representatives were viewed with suspicion by officials in the state machinery of these countries as well those that he visited as part of his two Asian expeditions. His endeavours, whether he wanted it or not, were inserted into the Great Game. He seems, however, to have negotiated the rocky terrain of mutually exclusive political relationships almost as well as he did the rocky terrain of the Himalayan and Altai ranges. His canvases on Shambhala and other Buddhist themes represented his utopic vision. He however also believed that Advent of the New Age was actually round the corner and that the ideal Buddhist state would be located somewhere between Tibet and Siberia. According to John McCannon, “...

recent scholarship has unearthed compelling body of evidence indicating that the Roerichs hoped to establish an independent—or at least quasi-autonomous—state in Tibet and the Himalayas, or alternatively, in southern Siberia and the Altai. In this 'Great Country', the Roerichs would construct a magnificent temple, preserve the cultural treasures of the world, and await the coming of Maitreya. How Russia, China, Mongolia—the nations in whose territory this latter-day Shambhala was to be reborn—might react to these plans seems not to have worried the Roerichs overmuch."[28] Marcus Osterrieder also points out that "Their ultimate objective—usually referred to as the 'Grand Plan' (*Velikij Plan*) was to establish a pan-Buddhist, transnational 'New Country' (*Novaya Strana*) stretching from Tibet to Southern Siberia, including territory that was governed by China, Mongolia, Tibet, and the Soviet Union. This 'New Country' was conceived as the manifest, earthly expression of the invisible Kingdom of Shambhala, 'the Holy Place, where the earthly world links with the highest states of consciousness'. Roerich's presumptuous ambition was nothing less than to prepare the coming of a New Age of peace and beauty, which would be ushered in by the earthly manifestation of Maitreya, the Buddha of the Future."[29]

Whatever Roerich's political ambitions, it is clear that Buddhism, the many legends and myths connected with it, created an imagined unitary space within Asia for him that was cultural but not overly political. In his paintings, he was a Modernist, a Symbolist, deeply linked by his work with the Silver Age of Russian culture; yet in his Modernism he moved away from the canons of the West. He created a parallel canon, in which the mountains and the caves signified the utopia of the future world of Shambhala. He transcended the Russian identity paradox of looking East or West, by overcoming the "otherness" of the East and making it a part of his own self.

Notes and References

1. A slightly different version of this paper was presented at the international conference on "Buddhism in Asia" organized by ICCR with the Embassy of India in Beijing in collaboration with Universities in China from 18-20 June 2011 at the Marriott Hotel, Beijing. A shorter version of this paper was presented at MAKAIAS in August 2011.
2. Madhavan Palat, "An Identity for Siberia," in *Asiatic Russia: Partnership and Communities in Eurasia*, S. Chatterjee, A. Sengupta, S. Bhattacharya (eds.) (Delhi: Shipra 2009), 10.
3. David S. Van Der Oye, "The East," in *A History of Russian Thought*, William Leatherbarrow, David Offord (eds.) (Cambridge: Cambridge University Press 2010), 231.
4. Ruth Coates, "Religious Renaissance in the Silver Age," in Leatherbarrow and Offord (eds.), *A History of Russian Thought*, 171.
5. Vsevolod Volodarsky, *Rerikh* (Moscow: Bely Gorod 2003), 7.
6. Bernice Glatzer Rozenthal, "Religious Humanism in the Russian Silver Age," in *The History of Russian Philosophy 1830–1930*, G M Hamburg, Randall A. Poole (eds.) (UK: Cambridge University Press 2010), 227.
7. Glatzer Rozenthal, "Religious Humanism," 228.
8. Judith Deutsch Kornblatt, "Eschatology and Hope in Silver Age Thought," in Hamburg and Poole (eds.), *The History of Russian Philosophy 1830–1930*, 286.
9. See Marcus Osterrieder, "From Synarchy to Shambhala: The Role of Political Occultism and Social Messianism in the Activities of Nikolai Roerich," 1 February 2007.
10. John McCannon, "Searching for Shambhala: The Mystical Art and Epical Journeys of Nikolai Roerich," *Russian Life* (January-February 2001): 50.

11. Nikolai Roerich, *The Heart of Asia* (Naggar, India: International Roerich Memorial Trust 2006), 68.
12. These include eschatological, spiritual, statist, anarchist, coercive, conversion-oriented, political-theocratic, ecclesiastical, perverted, cosmic, retrospective, erotic, Scythian, Slavophilian and Eurasian utopias.
13. Lyudmila Korotkina, *Tvorchesky Put' N Rerikha* (St Petersburg: ARS 2001), 148.
14. Roerich, *The Heart of Asia*, 74.
15. Madhavan Palat, "Nikolai Roerich: The Artist and the Messiah," handout distributed for the lecture delivered on 23 February 2010 at the international conference *Communities, Institutions and Transition in Post-1991 Eurasia*, MAKAIAS, Kolkata, 10.
16. Roerich, *The Heart of Asia*, 83.
17. Roerich, *The Heart of Asia*, 17.
18. "Roerich first met Agvan Dorjiev (Buryat lama who had close relations with Tsarist officials – RD) and heard his instructions about Shambhala in 1909, when he was a member of the construction committee of the new Buddhist Kalacakra sanctuary in St/ Petersburg." Osterrieder, "From Synarchy to Shambhala," 15.
19. Roerich, The *Heart of Asia*, 75.
20. Emanuel Sarkisyanz, "Communism and Lamaist Utopianism in Central Asia," *The Review of Politics* 20, no. 4 (October 1958): 630.
21. Roerich, The *Heart of Asia*, New York: Roevich Museum Press, 1929; Reprint by Pilgriors Publishing, 2007, 10.
22. Roerich, The *Heart of Asia*, 11.
23. Nikolai Roerich, *Shambhala* (New Delhi: Vedam 2003), 213.
24. See John McCannon's article on "Maeterlink" for a discussion on the links between the Gothic and Symbolist imagination.
25. Roerich, *Shambhala*, 42.
26. Osterrieder, "From Synarchy to Shambhala," 16–17.
27. Madhavan Palat, "Nikolai Roerich: The Artist and the Messiah," 14.
28. McCannon, "Searching for Shambhala," 52–53.
29. Osterrieder, "From Synarchy to Shambhala," 1.

3

Nicholas Roerich—A Quest and Legacy

Manju Kak

"To be close to Nicholas Roerich was like studying in several universities at the same time."

—Sina Fosdick

India has been as much the spiritual home of the Russian Roerich family, as much as Mother Russia. Clearly one of Russia's double-headed eagles faces east, a fact painter Nicholas Roerich (1874–1947) reminded his own countrymen of when Russian Court culture was heavily Francophone. From the time of his childhood spent in the family estate (reputedly once owned by an Indian Raja) "Isvara" *(Ishwara),* India was in his consciousness. And so it was befitting that Roerich died in December 1947, at Kullu, Himachal, India, where his simple grave lies under willows, marked by a monolithic rock that reads "Maharishi." But Roerich died without being able to return to his homeland, a citizen bereft of his nation.

For a painter-philosopher who never returned to Russia—having lived in India for twenty odd years—it is surprising that more than five hundred Roerich societies have proliferated since 1991 in the Russian Federation alone. They are dedicated to the propagation of Roerich's ideas as a peace activist (Roerich Peace Pact-1933) as well as the principles of his philosophical thought (Agni Yoga or Secret Doctrine of Living Ethics).

In the years following 1918 to 1991 Soviet Russia remained spiritually barren. The erstwhile communist leadership had closed doors firmly upon all organized religions. The more esoteric faiths and societies suffered a similar blackout, be it Buddhism, Theosophy, Agni Yoga, etc.[1] Particularly in the Stalinist years, Buddhist monasteries, schools, temples too were brutally destroyed and monks repressed. Nicholas and his wife, Helena Roerich's philosophy "Agni Yoga" drew much from these philosophies. It is said "The continuity of the theosophical outlook from Tsarist time to post communist Russia was established through Roerich."[2] Helena Roerich had translated two volumes of theosophist master H.P. Blavatsky's theosophical treatise "Secret Doctrine." After a long hiatus a resurgence of religiosity occurred in 1987 when the then Russian President Mikhail Gorbachev invited Nicholas Roerich's son Svetsolav to Moscow with the aim of establishing a Roerich Centre there.[3] Soon after a spiritual thaw set in. The law of the USSR "On Freedom of Conscience and Religious Organizations" was enacted in 1990. Amongst others the Russian Society of Theosophy too was restored in 1991, and UNESCO declared it the Year of H.P. Blavatsky. In the same year an International Council of Roerich Organizations was also founded. For Buddhists in Buryatiya, Tuva and Kalmykia, a new era began with the restoration of *datsans* and *dugans*, and the establishment of Buddhist-affiliated societies and associations. The doors had been flung open.

Subsequently, in October 1992, in Kazakhstan, the former republic of the Soviet Union, the First World Conference towards Spiritual Concord was organized at Almaty within the short span of 3 months; it was attended by 2500 participants. It is important to note it was organized through the International Association of Peace through Culture based in Moscow.[4] Roerich's concern for "Peace through Culture" was obscured through 1940s but interest remained through Roerich Societies in the West.

Since then many esoteric organizations have been revived or established in Russia including the Russian Society of Theosophy and the one devoted to the teaching of Roerichs' Agni Yoga or Living Ethics. Groups of devotees and admirers of the Roerich family legacy continue to spread across the Central Asian republics, America, Eastern Europe, Brazil, Argentina, Italy, France and above all India where he touched the Indian soul and made it resonate with Russian cadences. The present article indicates some of these vibrant resonances.

Early Life and Artistic Exposition

Though Roerich remained essentially Russian, he was a cosmologist, his consciousness belonging to an international arena. When fascist governments and monarchies were destroying Europe, visionaries like N. Roerich, Richard von Coudenhove-Kalergi (Pan-Europa), Henry Dunant (Red Cross) were presenting ideas that crossed national boundaries.

Roerich's life is mostly viewed in the larger collective of nineteenth and twentieth century western adventurers, colonial military agents and surveyors, and iconoclasts who thirsted for the unattainable far-off landscapes of the Orient. British army officer and explorer, Francis Younghusband, Nain Singh and Kishan Singh Rawat, Indian colonial surveyors who first mapped Tibet; Belgian French spiritualist and explorer, Alexandra David- Neel; Alexander Csoma de Koros, the Hungarian-Magyar wanderer and scholar; Albert Gruenwedel, the German Orientalist and explorer; Sven Hedin the Swedish scholar, were among those who explored and mapped much of Asia and around some of whom, cults have arisen.

Clearly in post-1991 Eurasia and beyond, Nikolai Konstantovich Roerich continues to arouse the interest of extensive scholarship, both adulatory and critical. Some give him the status of verily a demigod, while others relegate him to being a maverick, an adventurer with megalomaniacal delusions, a dabbler in spiritual ideas of unsubstantiated depth. Controversies aside, the question often asked is why? What is the draw and pull of a man who was in his final 'avatar' a painter of mountains?

Roerich's body of work has been divided into three periods by some critics, divisions that I look upon as progressing towards the same ideal, leading him down that one path.

His Russian period was called the "Stone" phase; it sought

to inquire into the common roots of the Russian peoples Slavic heritage, their pre-Christian, i.e. Celtic, Viking and Mongol traditions, and blood ties.[5] He raised awareness that this ancestry of old Russia should not to be forgotten and in this was deeply influenced by his teacher, the great Russian artist Archip Ivanovich Kuinji. Roerich was also close to some Slavophiles of the early 1900s, especially Princess Maria Teneshiva and her efforts at the experimental village, "Talashkino."

His second—theatrical—phase (especially in the 1920s) is seen in his oversized murals and decorative panels which express a continuum of inquiry into Russia's past, its animistic beliefs, its close unity with natural materials, implements and other objects. Association with theatre's luminaries such as Sir Thomas Beecham (Covent Garden) in England and Russian émigré impresario Sergei Diaghilev (Ballet Russes) and composer Igor Fyodorovich Stravinsky (Rites of Spring) made him renowned in Europe.

Finally his arrival in India on 30 November 1923 at Bombay was followed by his daring mountainous expeditions. The culmination of his quest was expressed in his transcendental paintings of the Himalayas and Trans-Himalayas, peopled with figures of enlightened saints, prophets, hierarchs, Keepers of the Spiritual Path; the nineteen-canvas "Banners of the East" series drawn from many faiths— Christ, Confucius, Moses, Buddha, Mohammed on Mt Hira, Lao-tse, Russia's own St. Sergius, the Buddhist Shambala kings, Rigden Gyalpo. As the Indian saint, Shri

Ramakrishna said, *Jata mat tata path*. Roerich too believed that all religions are paths to one God.

Through his body of work Roerich advocated a return to the ancient roots of human wisdom, which asserted the importance of spiritual life and of peaceful co-existence based on a cosmic mentality. Towards this end he linked these prophetic messages of Judeo-Christian and Islamic faiths with those of the older religious traditions of Asia and of the indigenous peoples of the Americas. Roerich believed Russian culture had very strong Indian roots.

Central Asian Expedition

It was this nascent quest—and the search for the elusive Buddhist mythological land of Shambhala that took Roerich upon his Central Asian Expedition (1924–28) across the Chinese Gobi desert and later into the Siberian Altai (1930–31). Ostensibly supported by American Secretary of Agriculture, Henry A. Wallace, (later Vice-President) as an Agrarian Expedition,[6] it had as its subtext this belief that "Shambala" did exist, a belief that was very similar to (the belief of) Belovodye, the land of Whitewater of Old Russian Believers who had fled to Siberia during church reforms of Patriarch Nikon (1652–66); the Christian Holy Grail; or the Hindu sacred geography of the mythical land of Meru.

Roerich's arrival in India was viewed with suspicion by the ruling British Raj authorities. This was a period of frenetic anti-Soviet activity stirred by the British colonial masters who were stakeholders in the "Great Game" being played out for dominance in Central and Inner Asia. To make matters worse Roerich quickly established friendship with many well-known Indian intellectuals such as Tagore, Suniti Kumar Chatterjee, Kedarnath Dasgupta, etc., and as time went by also continued to retain his Russian passport which made colonial rulers draw conclusions that he was a Comintern agent.

The route he took on his first expedition (1924–28) covered the vast and difficult geographical terrain of the Himalayas and of Central Asia, from Kashmir, Leh, Khotan, Kashgar, Urumchi, Mongolia, Gobi and Taklamakan deserts, to Tibet and finally Sikkim, a distance of over 8000 kms half the distance he was to travel. Roerich's philosophical ideas were honed and shaped by his great journeys.

He wished to learn about the origins of humanity. According to him Russia needed a detailed study of her eastern roots—the ethno-genesis and migration of peoples who came and filled and recreated Europe. His training in the Imperial Academy of Arts (1893) at St. Petersburg, and experience as an archaeologist came in handy. His jottings transferred to the books he wrote—*Altai-Himalaya, Heart of Asia*, etc., which form an important archive of happenings in Tibet, Mongolia, Buryatiya at that time, and how did it fit into the future of pre-World War II Eurasia.

The expeditions formed the "bridge" that connected his early explorations in Russia with his "arrival," in his new home in Kullu, (HP) and in the inter-disciplinary institute he set up "Urusvati." Here he hoped to diffuse the narrow pragmatic utilization of science, which lead to the destruction of nature, with a crucible of conscious knowledge that would save humanity, pin it to the domain of ethical science.

Roerich's first Central Asian Expedition formed the bedrock of the oeuvre of his paintings. Here he continued to express his "findings" till his death leaving behind a legacy of some 7000 paintings in museums and private collections the world over. He painted the majestic mountain peak, distant landscapes and peoples, together with their history, legends and spiritual traditions. He visualized the Himalayas and by extension the Trans-Himalayan region as a shared spiritual possession of many countries, peoples and faiths. In them he explored the language of colour that was both extraordinary and unique. He captured that spiritual dimension that has made the mountains home of the seeker, the sage and *rishi*. In his paintings Roerich expressed a core philosophy that spoke of *the* deep connectedness of man to nature and reinforced India's tradition for a culture of assimilation. Through them he reiterated an artist's belief that perfect worlds do exist, if only we could find the path to reach them. While he did not find "Shambhala," finally he knew it as state of the mind.

Following the expedition Roerich remained in India yet continued to straddle the "arc" that seeped into Russian consciousness in the severe communist decades, to remind her of her eastern heritage. This is the specific legacy that forms the bedrock of the societies that exist in his name.

Spiritual Quest

Most of Roerich's paintings were brought to cyber space post-

1991 because of the immense following he attracts. Yet in current and later western scholarship, Roerich has not been awarded his rightful place by the West in the world of art. The previous century was a time when western artists, connoisseurs, scholars had publically rejected spirituality and God. Roerich's work did not fit in into contemporary western trends. "He was not a cubist, fauvist, Dadaist, surrealist, or any other 'ist."[7] There was nothing here for the quest for the unknown found in Tibetan Buddhism or the Upanishads.

Another reason for this could be that there is often a marked difficulty expressed by western viewers in understanding Roerich's paintings.[8]

Possibly the average western viewer sees his work purely in the light of *mere* painting without its philosophic, esoteric connotation and contextualization. I use mere not to deny the elevated space of art, but to express a view that Roerich's oeuvre is "beyond art," i.e. not a *value* but a *dimension* or space easier understood by Indians whose everyday lives are indoctrinated by spiritual lacings.

In contrast, his work saw and continues to see unqualified admiration in India. His paintings quintessentially symbolize that which Indians hold close to their spiritual consciousness—the mighty Himalayas. Essentially Roerich's paintings demonstrate the power of human consciousness to penetrate the fundamental unity of things. In a sense they seek to ask what our connectedness to the impulse that created us is. The fulcrum of Roerich's entire body of work lies in just such subtle messages that are imbued with history of civilization, the connection with the divine, to many lives.

They are rooted in the ancient *aranya* texts that uphold the keel of nature which economists now acknowledge as indispensable to the future basis of world civilization. They also display what Buddhist scholar Andrea Loseries calls a unique luminosity. Roerich himself said "Culture is the worship of light."

Roerich captured landscapes where man was alone and dominated by cosmic forces. According to him wild "untouched spaces like the Siberian taiga—mountains, glaciers, rivers, lakes—were sanctuaries, the life source of civilization—vital organs of the earth that need protection and care, to remain so," says Prof. A.V. Ivanov.[9] Alas, man has reached everywhere; there are fewer and fewer wild spaces left, inaccessible regions are in jeopardy. The cognition of beauty is what will save mankind, said Dostoevsky. Concurs L.V. Shaposhnikova, "when we are exploring our consciousness of cosmic space the Oneness of Nature manifests as taught in Indian spiritual texts of the Vedanta and Upanishads. As much as political boundaries separate, it is the awareness of the contiguous bonds of air, space and water that bind."[10] "Thought is the core of our evolution," says Shaposhnikova. "Today to work in co-operation it is important to foster supra-national thinking."

In Moscow, a central focus for the International Centre for Roerichs is the establishment of a Centre for Cosmic Thinking. It seeks to address just such a cause, the connectedness of all life, and the implications of the mystic law of Cause and Effect, the *dharma chakra parivartana* of Buddhists. It is said the biggest challenge to this century is the quest for universal peace, sustainable ecology and the eradication of poverty. Nature cannot thrive without peace. The Hindu sages of the Upanishads uttered *Pritvi Shantih, Antariksha Shantih, Om! Shantih Shantih Shantih* which was echoed in Roerich's "Where there is culture, there is peace." Culture is heart and cosmic laws are perhaps more visible through the creative work of men which form the crossing of three worlds—the terrestrial world, the world of ideas and of spirit.

Preservation of Culture—Roerich Peace Pact

The architectural quality of Roerich's work is seen in his paintings, "Island of Rest," "Great Spirit of the Himalaya," etc. His symbolism is evocative. Both in his paintings and his work as an archaeologist, his concern for buildings, ancient churches and city walls show his concern for material culture.

In post 1991 Eurasia, International Roerich Societies emphasize the protection of just such material architecture and cultural heritage in times of war, natural disaster, and armed conflict through seminars and publications. After the Iraq National Museum was looted (2003), the Kabul Museum defaced and Bamyan Buddhas obliterated in Afghanistan (2001), in Serbia Mostar's sixteenth century Stari Most across Neretva River was destroyed in Croatian attack (1993), and in India the Babri Masjid was demolished two decades ago, the reverberations of which we still feel. Thus, Roerich's global ideas on cultural preservation have acquired greater significance in this new century. In Russia too paradoxically while the Russians preserved Moscow's legacy of Tsarist buildings, today as new wealth dominates this luxury-crazed city, worries over the preservation of historic architecture loom large.

Between the decades 1940 to 1990 we have destroyed fifty per cent of our cultural heritage, says Archduke Karl von Hapsburg-Lothringen, President of the International Committee of the Blue Shield.[11] In the past, international or national conflicts targeted infrastructure. But today when strife is increasingly based on ethnicity, cultural property becomes the object of rage. From the Russo-Japanese War (1905) onwards, the early twentieth century was devastated by war on a scale not seen before leaving the world fraught with paranoia. Europe and by extension Russia lived in a cauldron of hate and destruction till the outbreak of the two World Wars.

Clearly cultural property is non renewable. It has always been believed that artists have a special calling for they are particularly sensitive to the cause of culture. It was during his student years, that Roerich began working for world peace. Even before the Bolshevik Revolution broke out Roerich had already laid his ground work for activity through his mobilizing of artists. Here he held a number of positions that were to prepare him for the leadership he showed later.

Roerich had gained a reputation in imperialist Russia as a painter, archaeologist, philosopher, but once the Bolshevik Revolution of 1917 gained ground, he left Russia foreseeing the Soviet policy of controlling all art forms for narrow political purposes. The family departed to Sweden, London and then to America. During the Stalinist years Roerich lived in Paris and America, and later India.

His artistic response to world events came through his paintings titled, "The Cry of the Serpent," "The Doomed City," "The Crowns," "The Lurid Glare," "Human Deeds." It was 1929—when he had settled down in India that he proposed the Peace Pact Committee—and the Roerich Banner of Peace. The Roerich Peace Pact Committee was based in New York. He had set up the Master School of United Arts, Cor Ardens, Corona Mindi, and later Roerich Museum, Roerich Museum Press, and allied institutions while in America.[12] The Banner of Peace— a kind of Red Cross symbol—was a white flag with three magenta spheres enclosed in a circle that are said to represent science, religion and art, also to symbolize the past, the present, the future, in the overarching circle of eternity.

At the time of the Second World War, an effort to make nations responsible for culture was made by Roerich through a gathering of artists, scientists, teachers, priests, politicians from 35 countries who met at the mediaeval city of Bruges, Belgium, to give their endorsement to these ideas. Roerich proposed what came to be known as the Roerich Pact, which calls for the protection and preservation of cultural values during wartime. On 14 April 1935 the Pact was signed in Washington at the White House by President F.D. Roosevelt and 20 Latin American countries of the Pan American Union. The articles of the Pact are based on a document drafted by Georges Chklaver, doctor of international law and political science at the University of Paris. Here Roerich's training as a lawyer was of added support. Later in India, the 6th All India Cultural Unity Conference in Calcutta (Kolkata) resolved to adopt the Pact—and in 1948 the newly formed Indian Government agreed to adopt it as well.

The contribution of the Roerich Pact to the articles of the 1954 Hague Convention for the Protection of Cultural Property in the Event of Armed Conflict and recently to the Second Protocol of 1999, both of which form the basis of our cultural treaties, is well documented. But, though 1954 Hague Convention prohibits the deportation of cultural property from the region, many states do not have the requisite legal framework to protect this. International law can only establish framework for legislation, but measures have to be taken nationally to make it a ground reality.[13]

Shambhala—Land of Dharma

As mentioned earlier, Roerich's influences were largely from eastern philosophies. In 1901, Nicholas Roerich married Helena, born in an accomplished St. Petersburg family. She shared his interest in art, music and the philosophy of China, Tibet and India and possessed immense knowledge of Buddhist philosophy.

The young couple cooperated with the Buryat Lama Dorzhiev in building a Tibetan Buddhist Temple in St. Petersburg. Dorzhiev saw the possibility of an alliance of the Buriats, Kaimyk and other Buddhist tribes living in the eastern part of Russia with the thirteenth Dalai Lama, who was the most politically aware of the Dalai Lamas then. From

Dorzhiev, the Roerichs learned of the Tibetan text and ritual, the *Kalachakra* (The Wheel of Time) and of the coming of a new historical-astrological cycle "The New Age" to be marked by a new Buddha, Maitreya.

Contemporary scholars hold that Roerich's own spiritual and philosophical aspirations are said to have been towards the establishment of a neo-Buddhists state in which Russia would have a place, one that would place it firmly as an eastern power. Tsar Nicholas II as the Buddhist Tsar would have been a counter weight to English and Chinese influence in Tibet before plans fell through and the Bolsheviks drove the family of Romanovs out of Soviet Russia.

Much of this has come under speculation of post-*perestroika* scholars who imbue it as a grand territorial ambition, his larger than life obsession, but Roerich's admirers have always said he was a visionary, an objective I hold true.

Roerich's defenders claim that his pursuit was for a land of "dharma"—the physical manifestation of a veritable Shambhala, where man could return to the earth its pristine and divine beauty, protect its isolated prairies, allow for nature to breathe. Therefore he made his repeated assertion that "Beauty is Culture." For him the anti-imperialist movement could provide an excellent opportunity to carve a pan Mongol space or a pan Buddhist space—where such a cultural and philosophical environment could be the bridge between a Tsarist and new Russia. Roerich's understanding for this is marked in his diaries and writings.

It is to be remembered between the wars—the conflicting ramifications of universal socialist ideas were permeating propelling the growth of peoples' movements in China, India and Russia in the same time frame—the question often asked was what shape and role should the Americans carve for themselves? Roerich sought perhaps to show them a direction that re-enforced his earlier mentioned quest. His rolc as a political iconoclast is fiercely debated—but it maybe outside the perception and understanding of linear political thought.

It is said failure is a step towards victory. Failure nowhere lessened the strength of Roerich's belief, and his legacy in stressing the importance of Russia's eastern lands. Motives of artists are not easily understood; how their *seemingly* conflicting thoughts and ideas fuse upon a central goal. Says the Nobel laureate and writer Orhan Pamuk, men have the capacity to entertain contradictory thoughts with much more capacity than nineteenth century writings have told us is possible.[14] That we do not have to follow them sequentially, or for them to be in logical progression, for the mind to sift them and perceive their connectivity. Often, what seems like contradictions or vacillation is really propelled by this 'tree' thinking.

Roerich continued to watch the international scenario develop between the '30s and '40s from his perch in the mountains of Kullu in India, still with his Russian passport, quintessentially not ceasing to consider himself a *bonafide* Russian.

At this point again Roerich's paintings were considered in some way to be prophetic. For example "Gesar Khan," "News from the Himalayas," "News from the North," "Igor's Nation." In 1941, amidst Soviet army defeat "Alexander Nevsky" rides in the middle of a battlefield of soldiers.

Indian Legacy

Roerich believed Russian culture had very strong Indian roots and that the world too was indebted to Indian philosophical and cultural traditions. Scholars such as Prof. John McCannon write of Roerich's "western dismay" when he first arrived on seeing Indian poverty and the abysmal conditions of people under British rule, but those outcries are bedded midst other observations where the "*apna pan*" of self-critique is clear. Roerich did love India, unequivocally, but he did see the inequities, the degradation, and he makes mention of an India chaffing under the British yoke, as if was his own will that was colonized.

But cultural values we cherish are often translated through the works, ideas, and practices, of painters, poets, writers and architects. Both Russia and India are old souls. In their quest for modernity they shared the same time line. When Tsarist Russia went to war with Japan, there were reverberations in India in the Partition of Bengal (1905). As the Bolshevik Revolution gained ground, the Khilafat movement boosted the nascent Indian Congress Party. From Gandhi's early correspondence with Leo Tolstoy to Pandit Nehru's socialist sympathies dating from when he visited the Soviet Union in 1927 and Indo-Russian friendship blossomed. Later, the Indian public sector was developed in synchronicity with what he saw (BHEL, SAIL, etc). Diplomatic ties too were formulated even before we became independent in 1947.

As an internationalist Roerich shared with Nehru consensual thoughts on the international events of the time. His friendship emphasized and added to "Nehruvian Vision" in its important and formative years, the extra dimension of the Himalayan spiritual heritage. The same relevance remains today in dealing with contemporary challenges in these fragile ecospheres.

Today Roerich's legacy strengthens the case for India's traditions for composite culture and internationalism. Innumerable inspirational paintings of Roerich are found at museums and institutes in Banaras, Chandigarh, Delhi (Pusa), Allahabad, Madras and Naggar aside from those in private collections. The International Roerich Memorial Trust is headquartered in Bangalore (India) and at Naggar, Kullu. At a time when, post 9/11 religious and ethnic strife are tearing apart Eurasia, and Central and South Asia, and the world is increasingly being viewed as bi-polar, and sometimes even unipolar, Roerich's work, rooted in the sense of common religious beliefs and shared cultures, is relevant in our increasingly fragmented society.

Through his paintings, the Roerich Peace Pact, his delving into the philosophy of Living Ethics, his journeys, one thing comes true and clear is that he was looking for the essential unity of life, its intermingling with a common universal soul.

True post-1991, together with a parallel development of relationships with the Central Asian Republics, a new extraordinary scenario has emerged. But as the declarations of the tenth year of Indo-Russian strategic partnership have shown (in areas to combat nuclear and other terror, military armament, and space exploration, gas exploration, defense, energy, science and technology), it is important, to keep Russia-India cultural bonding alive and vibrant in its shared spiritual and philosophical space that the Roerich family's body of work envisioned.

Notes and References

1. The Soviet Government flatly forbade theosophy and the association of Russian theosophist. A few members were forced to emigrate abroad after 1938. www.hctheosophist.com/archives/pdf/hc200301.pdf, p3.2/9/2011.
2. www.hctheosophist.com/archives/pdf/hc200301.pdf,p3,2/9/2011
3. Raisa Gorbachev was involved in starting a fund in the name. www.hctheosophist.com/archives/pdf/hc200301.pdf, p4, 2/9/2011.
4. Report of "First World Congress towards Spiritual Concord," Alma Ata, October 1992 (Transnational Associations 43, 1993): 28–37.
5. It is interesting to note Roerich's mother had Mongol blood.
6. http://www.thehindu.com/thehindu/fline/f2625/stories/20091218262509200.htm 5/22/2010.
7. www.hctheosophist.com/archives/pdf/hc200301.pdf. 2/9/2011.
8. Though conversely they have begun commanding an exorbitant price amongst art dealers and collectors the world over.
9. Barnaul University, Russian Federation.
10. The 2010 Europa Nostra, Europe's foremost prize for culture was awarded to Mme Shaposhnikova for making the dilapidated Lopukhins Estate into one of the finest museums dedicated to N. Roerich's work both as a painter and cultural/peace activist. Established in 1963, EUROPA NOSTRA represents 400 organizations across Europe and is headed by the Spanish tenor Placido Domingo.
11. Established in 1996, the "Blue Shield" Committees aim to be for cultural heritage what the Red Cross is to human life.
12. Sina Fosdick, "Letters," *Meeting My Master*, New York, 7 July 1948.
13. Maria Teresa Dutli, *Celebrating 75 years of the Roerich Peace Pact*, Seminar Proceedings, International Centre for Roerichs, Moscow, 8–11 October 2010.

14. Orhan Pamuk, *The Naïve and Sentimental Novelist* (New Delhi: Penguin India 2010).

For further reading please see

John Snelling, *Buddhism in Russia: The Story of Agvan Dorzhiev, Lhasa's Emissary to the Tsar* (Rockport, Mass.: Element Books 1993).

David Schimmelpenninck van der Oye, *Russian Orientalism* (New Haven: Yale University Press 2010).

Jaquelene Decter, *Nicholas Roerich: The Life and Art of a Russian Master*, Inner Traditions International and Nicholas Roerich Museum, 1989.

Nicholas Roerich, *The Heart of Asia* (New York: Roerich Museum Press 1929, reprint in Varanasi: Pilgrims Publishing 2007).

Nicholas Roerich, *Altai-Himalaya: A Travel Diary* (London: Jarrolds Publishers, n.d.).

Nicholas Roerich, *Himalayas- Adobe of Light* (London: David Marlowe 1947).

Nicholas Roerich, *Maitreya* (New York: 1932, reprint by IRMT, Naggar, Kullu 2006).

Nicholas Roerich, *The Invincible* (New York: Nicholas Roerich Museum, 1974).

4
Tibetan Buddhist Monks and Monasteries in Contemporary Buryatiya

Tsymzhit P. Vanchikova

The era of globalization, industrialization and information have created challenges to which all religions have responded with innovative discourses. This also can be said about Buddhism. Especially it concerns the countries with changing political systems, among them we have to mention former socialist countries like Mongolia. Substantial developments within societies, such as improved technology, science, urbanization and increasing economic security have a strong influence on the changes within the Buddhist church itself. As far as it concerns the theme of the article, Buddhism in Russia has been undergoing several changes from the first quarter of the twentieth century up to the present time and was characterized by several specific features caused by certain historical circumstances.

Buddhism in contemporary Buryatiya and the religious situation in general provides scholars with unique opportunity of analysing various institutions and their development. The present development of new institutions, their responses to socio-political changes, and their factual manifestations allows eyewitnesses to experience events that have taken place during the initial stages of the post-Soviet period.

The paper will give a preliminary survey of the history of settlement of Tibetan monks in contemporary Buryatiya. This process is quite unique and there are remarkable features in the multi-dimensional process. Owing to patience and persistence of elderly Buddhist monks who have been released after a long period of imprisonment or exile, owing to the leaders' association with the Buddhist church of Buryatiya and the former USSR, the traditions of Buddhism, Buddhist ethics have been preserved among the believers. The process of revival of Buddhism started in 1990 after the issue of Russian "Law on freedom of confession." The Buddhist church as well as other religious confessions was given help and assistance in gradual rebirth of monastic religious activities and educational system. With the emergence of new generation of young educated Buryat monks the life in Buddhist monasteries gradually acquired steady features of independent internal self-organization, corresponding to traditional standards of former monastic discipline and learning. Besides many changes in Buryat Buddhism we can mention quite a new phenomenon namely the appearance of Tibetan monks and Tibetan temples in Buryatiya.

First Tibetans in Buryatia

In this article, the history of relations between Tibetan monks and the Buryat population as well as their influence on the local population will be studied. To begin with, a short history of former relationship between Tibetans and the Buryat people is being given here. Buddhism was brought to Buryatiya by several Mongol chieftains who escaped from Mongolia and came and settled in Buryatiya with their kinsmen during 1620–1760.[1] They came along with their Buddhist monks who started to conduct first sermons in felt yurts. They settled down and intermixed with the local people. The Buryats became interested in Buddhist teaching, received primary knowledge from the newcomers, took Buddhist oaths and vows. The process of Buddhist penetration was slow but steady. Later Buryat lamas themselves went to the monasteries of Mongolia and Tibet for studying. The earliest known contacts of the Buryat people with the Tibetans can be traced to the beginning of the eighteenth century.

Buryat historical records have very scanty information about this time. Thus in the earliest records of Toboev and Yumsunov we find data about the arrival of 150 Tibetan and Mongolian lamas in 1712 who fled to Buryatiya escaping military suppression in Mongolia and Tibet.[2] They wandered among different Buryat ethnic groups, mainly in the border areas, and preached Buddhist teaching. Some of them became the first abbots of the first Buryat Buddhist temples, for example Agvan Puntsok and Lubsan Sheirab.[3] Also, we find information that lamas from Mongolia and Tibet often travelled to Transbaikal region especially in the second half of the nineteenth and the beginning of the twentieth centuries. They preached various religious sermons in different Buddhist monasteries.[4] The Tibetan monks were mostly from Amdo region in Tibet—that is why monks of most of Buryat monastic schools studied according to the syllabus of the monasteries of that region. Among them mentioned are several high ranked lamas from north-west Tibet.[5]

Many oral accounts transmitted by Buryat elders tell us about huge amount of goods, cattle and money donated to them by the believers. This testifies the fact that Tibetan monks were quite popular among the Buryat population and were respected by them. According to the available data we can say that the relations between Tibetan monks and Buryats were quite stable and more or less regular. The more so as Buryat monks and pilgrims used to go for pilgrimage to holy Buddhist places of Mongolia, Tibet and by the end of the nineteenth and beginning of the twentieth century to China and India. This process ceased after the October Revolution. From the end of '30s of the twentieth century, with the onset of the Stalinist purges, Buddhism officially ceased to exist, all monasteries were destroyed, lamas were arrested and sent to concentration camps. It cannot be said that people completely obeyed the authorities, though believers were deprived of the possibility of public expression of their belief in temples, Buddhism prevailed as a way of life by the elders in the families and in popular consciousness.

A New Phase in Tibeto-Buryat Relations

After World War II, slight changes in the policy towards religion began. In 1945 it was allowed to reopen Aginskii and rebuild Ivolginskii *datsans*. Although this did not mean a change in general policy towards religion, at least Buddhism in Buryatiya was allowed to exist as an officially recognized religion. Beside these two centres of religion, where up to 20 monks were allowed to stay, dozens of monks who were freed from concentration camps illegally served in villages almost in all regions of Buryatiya. By 1970 only a few elder lamas remained. So till the beginning of *perestroika* there were only two functioning Buddhist monasteries that were under strict state control.

Since *perestroika*, some juridical actions were taken to empower Buryat citizens with constitutional rights of freedom of belief. After the liberal law of 1990 of Soviet President Gorbachev on the freedom of conscience, the religious situation in Russia began to change. Religious confessions almost eradicated during the Soviet period were revived. It was accompanied by active process of restoration of destroyed temples, the revival of forgotten religious traditions and rituals in everyday life of the people. This process was connected with the increase of national self-consciousness and with the search of ethnic roots and Buddhism was considered to be one of the main fundamental pillars of national culture and identity.[6] At present there are 203 registered different Buddhist organizations in Russia, among them 56 are registered in Buryatiya.

This time the contacts with Tibetans were laid down by several visits of His Holiness Dalai Lama, the first being in 1979. During the first visit he discussed with Buryat Buddhist leaders the problem of revival of Buddhism that greatly depended on teaching and preparing younger generation of monks. This became possible since 1990 and 1991 when 2 Buddhist schools were opened at Aginski and Ivolginski *datsans* and several Tibetan monks were sent by Dalai Lama to serve as teachers at these schools. The most important step in this direction has been done about 20 years ago in accordance with kind permission of His Holiness Dalai Lama when dozens of young Buryat boys have been sent to Tibetan Buddhist monasteries in India, to be trained in Dharamsala and Goman/Drepung monasteries. Now more than 50 students study there.

For teaching in these Buryat Buddhist schools, which were later transformed into institutes, well-educated Tibetan monks were sent by His Holiness the Dalai Lama. During these years the number of monks has not only increased but also the best among them continue education at Tibetan Buddhist monasteries in India for several years and return to Buryatia. Now there are about 1000 monks in all Buryat monasteries, according to the data given by the Buryat head monk Damba Ayusheev to the Council for Religious Affairs of the Government of Buryatiya, but this data seems to be exaggerated.

Buddhism in Buryatiya is represented practically by all its main schools and denominations. Thus not only the teachings of the traditional Gelugpa School, some other schools of Buddhism, like Nyingma, Kargyu, Karma, Sakya have started spreading. The Tibetan esoteric institution, Dzogchen is also becoming quite popular. In 1990s the top hierarchy of all the four main Tibetan Buddhist schools has visited Buryatiya as well as many high-ranked Tibetan monks. In general there is a special kind attitude and interest towards all Tibetans from the side of the Buryat people. It has historic roots, as all Tibetans are associated with the name of the Dalai Lama and Tibet itself, which was traditionally considered by Buryat believers to be a holy land inhabited by gods. Buddhists of Buryatiya have restored close relations with Buddhist communities of Mongolia and Tibet among which there are Tibetan monks who have been educated in India. Buddhists of Buryatia are quite active in some international political issues, in particular, the status of Tibet. Associations like "Society of Friends of Tibet," "Green Tara," Agvan Dorzhiev's foundation, "Aryabala" promote active propaganda in support of the struggle of "Tibetan people for independence from communist China."

Tibetan Monks in Contemporary Buryatiya

Of special interest is the missionary work of Tibetan refugee monks. Since 1993 Tibetan monks regularly came for teaching Buddhist courses and helping in the restoration of some religious sermons and rituals, like tantric and meditative practices as well as the *Kalachakra* tantric practice, etc. We witness quite a new phenomenon in Buryatiya that is connected with the process of migration and naturalization of Tibetan monks in Buryatiya and appearance of Buddhist monasteries built and run by Tibetans. This time the movement is represented by Tibetans born in India, mostly by the second generation of Tibetan refugees.

The Buryat traditional *sangha* is anxious with the influx of religious personalities from abroad, especially from the side of the Indian Tibetan emigrants. Tibetan refugee monks quite successfully conduct missionary work among the believers while Buryat Buddhist monks are not active in this aspect and that is why traditional Buddhist *sangha* of Russia (mainly the Khambo lama Damba Ayusheev) disapproves the activities of Tibetan Buddhist monks and organizations. This was openly declared by Khambo Lama in newspapers[7] several times. This has become a reason for competition with Tibetan monks.

At the first stage after coming to Buryatiya Tibetans served at Buryat Buddhist temples together with Buryat lamas. Gradually they acquired their own followers and believers and began to form a niche and be integrated into the society. With this, the question of their official status in Russia has cropped up. Those Tibetan lamas who wanted to stay in Buryatiya began to look for the ways of doing it and to receive Russian citizenship. It is known that Russian citizenship can be received in accordance with the requirements of the Federal Law "About citizenship of Russian Federation" issued on 31 May 2002 and the President's Decree no. 1325, from 14 November 2002. It is quite a complicated bureaucratic procedure like in any other country. In order to receive a Russian passport a person has to live with residence permit in Russia for 5 years without going out of the country, he has to pass an exam in Russian and to testify that he can earn money for living. There are several exceptions such as marriage to a Russian citizen. As far as they are concerned, the Tibetans are looking for ways of naturalization. Some of the Tibetans received citizenship before the issuing the law when the requirements were not so strict; some have received it in Kalmykia, where Buddhism was supported by the President Kirsan Ilyumzhinov and that is why it was much easier than in any other place; some of them marry local girls in order to obtain legitimate rights for staying in Russia. Some of them live with temporal documents, i.e. residence permits. Those with Russian passports can freely travel in Russia and abroad and lead active religious work.

Some of the Tibetan monks are very popular and have lots of disciples. Particularly important are Elo-Rinpoche and Geshe Tinley. Eshe-Lodoi Rinpoche or Elo Rinpoche is considered to be the fourth incarnation of Elo-tulku and is a well educated Tibetan Buddhist monk. He entered monastic school of Gomang philosophical faculty of Gomang monastery at the age of 6. He escaped from Tibet to India in 1959. From 1959 to 1969 he lived in the Buxa Duar in West Bengal. At the age of 20 he received monastic vows from His Holiness the Dalai Lama. From 1969 to 1971, he lived in Dharamsala and worked there as a head librarian at the Tibetan works and archives. In 1979 Eshe Lodoi Rinpoche obtained the philosophic degree of *geshe-lharampa* at Gomang monastery in India. In 1991 he was sent by the Dalai Lama to Mongolia where he was teacher at the Buddhist University at Gandantekchenling monastery. In 1993 he was invited to Buryatiya for restoration of Buddhist monastic education and Buddhist religious tradition. In 1997 Elo Rinpoche received Russian citizenship and settled down in Ulan-Ude. He has built one of the largest Buddhist temples in Ulan-Ude that is supposed to become a new centre for the further dissemination of Buddhism in the region. He regularly gives lectures and performs different types of initiations for his disciples or sometimes lectures on general Buddhist theory and practice. He visits different parts of Russia for missionary purposes.

Another Tibetan Buddhist monk, geshe Jampa Tinley, the former representative of His Holiness the Dalai Lama to Russia came to Russia for the first time in April 1993 and in 1998 received Russian citizenship. Geshe Jampa Thinley was born in 1962 in South India in the family of Tibetan refugees. He has graduated from the Central Institute of higher Tibetan studies in Sarnath and received shastri degree. In 1994 he became a *geshe*—doctor of Buddhist philosophy. At the age of 25 received monk's vows. In 1993 he was sent to Russia by His Holiness Dalai Lama as his representative. Since this time all his life is closely connected with Russia and Buryatia and the revival and development of Buddhism. Due to his active missionary work he has acquired many followers all over Russia. He is a spiritual leader of several Buddhist dharma centres, such as Moscow Buddhist centre of lama tsonkapa, Chenrezi centre in Elista, Manjusri centre in Kyzyl, Tara centre in Omsk, Atisha centre in Irkutsk, Maitreya in Novosibirsk, Tushita in Ufa, etc. All his lectures have been published. In 2004 he disrobed and continues his missionary activities. He knows English and has learnt Russian quite well. In one of his interviews to local Buryat newspaper, he mentioned that his main task is to help to the revival of Buddhism and Buddhist education for monks, to create

Dharma centres for the laymen. Due to his proselytizing activities, he has acquired lots of disciples all over Russia. The texts of his sermons and lectures have been published in Russian in large editions.

Judging from the activities of Buddhist missionaries in Russia, as well as in Buryatiya we see the emergence not only of a large quantity of believers, but of certain communities of educated and secular intellectuals, who are interested in Buddhist teaching, united by the same spiritual teacher.

Tibetan Monasteries in Ulan-Ude

There about 20 Tibetans in Buryatiya serving mostly at four Buddhist temples built by Tibetan monks. Most of them serve at monasteries and small religious centres organized either by themselves or by Buryat monks. Some Tibetan monks rent houses and organize small temples in them, like Tibetan lama Genden Gyaltsen (his temple is named as Gundelling). There is no strict attachment to that or this monastery, some of the monks freely serve in several temples together with Buryat monks, often go with religious purposes to different regions of Buryatiya or cities of Russia.

The largest of the temples is the temple of a regional Buddhist organization Tibetan Cultural Centre called "Rinpoche bagsha," an independent religious organization that was organized in 2000, registered on 25 January 2001. "Bagsha" is a Buryat word for Indian guru or teacher. The chairman of the centre and the head monk of the temple is a Tibetan Rinpoche (Elo Tulku) – Eshe Lodoi Elo Rinpoche.

As per the registration documents, its main purpose is to conserve and to spread classical Buddhist teaching and culture of Gelugpa tradition. In 2000 the construction of a new temple was begun by Elo Rinpoche and his disciple geshe-lharamba Tenzin-lama in Ulan-Ude. Elo Rinpoche received the Dalai Lama's permission to erect a temple. It was completed with financial help from different organizations, state and municipal, as well as by numerous followers of Rinpoche and donations.

There are approximately 20 monks in this monastery; 3-5 of them are Tibetans. The centre publishes its newspaper (*Migjed*) and in 2010 it has created its own website.[8] The temple is being enlarged gradually. The largest statue of Golden Buddha was enshrined in the main temple in 2004, and in 2005 eight stupas have been built; in 2009 a large Buddhist bell was set up. Within a short period of time the temple of Elo Rinpoche became an important religious centre for numerous pilgrims and believers.

Another large monastery has been built by geshe Jampa Tinley.[9] They have built a temple in Ulan-Ude and are building an all-Russian Baikal retreat centre not far from Lake Baikal. In Ulan-Ude he works in close cooperation with Green Tara community.[10] Quite popular among the believers are Tibetan medical centres, such as Buddhist medical temple or centre, named as "Sorig oiling". This religious community was founded in 2004 by Yamphel-lama (Yamphel Dondup Ganphel Jigme). In 2006 this group has built a new large building for the centre, which serves as a Buddhist temple also. There are approximately 3-4 Tibetans in this centre.

All Tibetan temples work autonomously, and most of them have their own parish and parishioners, though other people can freely visit them and address their monks. There is no rigid attachment to this or that temple. On special occasions, for example, on Tibetan New Year, all Tibetan monks come to the temple of Elo Rinpoche and exchange greetings and also participate in religious sermons. Also Tibetans gather during large religious ceremonies at the temple of Elo-Rinpoche on invitation. The spiritual authority of Elo Rinpoche is recognized by all Tibetans here.

Conclusion

There are several reasons for the success of Tibetan activity in Buryatiya.

1. In contrast to their missionary work in the West, Buddhism in Buryatiya has been a living tradition and has been preserved by the people, especially by the older generation. Despite decades of atheist persecution it was one of the driving forces of national consciousness since *perestroika*. This made their mission much simpler.
2. Tibetan monks were most needed for restoring broken links of Buddhist tradition related to transmission of knowledge and teaching skills from the teacher to his pupil. They participated in the revival of most monastic sermons and rituals.
3. The Tibetans through more than half a century of

immigration and residence in a foreign linguistic and ethnic environment, have not only acquired experience of survival, but also improved methods of preaching and missionary work. They have successfully adapted to the complexities of Buddhist teaching, presenting them in a simple and easy way for comprehension. That is why they managed to organize their circle of followers and believers in Buryatiya relatively quickly.

4. Many Tibetan teachers can deliver their lectures in English. Moreover, the lamas who settled in Buryatiya successfully master the Buryat and Russian languages through which communication with people is easier.

We can conclude that Tibetan monks took an active part in restoration of Buddhism in Buryatiya. Tibetans, as well as Buddhist monks and lay people, have adapted themselves and their monasteries quite well to the modern society, and this is significant if we take into consideration the fact that earlier they lived in secluded monasteries of India. Tibetan diasporization for those who became Russian citizens in Buryatiya as well as in Russia in general has also yielded results for the Buddhist community in Russia.

Notes and References

1. Sh. B. Chimitdorzhiev and Ts. P. (eds.), *Buryatskie Letopisi* (Buryat Historical Records) (Ulan-Ude 1996).
2. T. Toboev, "*Proshlaya istoriya khorinskikh i aginskikh buryat*" (Early History of Qori and Aga Buryats) in Chimitdorzhiev and

Ts. P. (eds.), *Buryatskie Letopisi*, 15; V. Yumsunov, "Istoriya proiskhozhdeniya 11 khorinskikh rodov" (The history of origin of 11 khori tribes), in Chimitdorzhiev and Ts. P. (eds.), *Buryatskie Letopisi*, 43; G.D. Natsov, *Materialy po Lamaizmu v Buryatii* (Materials on Lamaism in Buryatia) (Ulan-Ude 1998), 31.

3. Toboev, *Proshlaya istoriya*, 15; Yumsunov, "Istoriya proiskhozhdeniya," 43, 46; Natsov, *Materialy po Lamaizmu v Buryatii*, 6.
4. Natsov, *Materialy po Lamaizmu v Buryatii*, 139–41.
5. Natsov, *Materialy po Lamaizmu v Buryatii*, 56–58, 111, 127–29.
6. Buddhism was not the only component for the revival of national self-consciousness and national identity. They were also based on shamanism, revival of the all-Mongolian idea of Chingis-khan and folk hero Geser.
7. For example in one of his interviews to the question about ethnic relations in Buryatia he answered: "In Ulan-Ude there became too many Tibetan monks. They left their monasteries in Tibet and India, this is not good. Lamas must not leave their monasteries." *Informpolis*, Ulan-Ude, 26 January 2011.
8. Available from http://elo-rinpoche.ru/
9. Available from http://www.geshe.ru/
10. Green Tara (Nogoon Dara eke) is an independent religious organization in Ulan-Ude. This community of Buddhists was registered on 01.07.1999. The head of the community is getsulma (Buddhist nun) Tenzin Choidron. Her lay name is Irina S. Urbanaeva, she is a doctor of philosophy and works at the IMBT SB RAS. This community was founded by the initiative of geshe Jampa Tinley.

5
Situating Pilgrimage: Evaluating the Role of Myanmar Monasteries in South Asia

Swapna Bhattacharya (Chakraborti)

Myanmar as Pilgrim Destination

It has been a unique experience in writing this paper; a major part of this work is based on my experience of field research in Bihar, UP and Lumbini in Nepal. I undertook this field work during the period from April 2009 to November 2009, the results of which have been published as Occasional Paper entitled *India and Myanmar: People, Pilgrimage, Histories and the Present.*[1] I have visited various monasteries, old and new. Among the new ones are those that are now coming up in places like Bodhgaya and Delhi. There are now at least two monasteries by Arakanese monks, one by the Shans besides the main Myanmar monastery. For my writings that are based on field research material, I have dealt with those major Myanmar monasteries in which I have lived and enjoyed the hospitality of the venerable Sayadaws. Therefore, the well known Myanmar monasteries in each of these two states of India and Lumbini were pivotal to my investigation. During the pilgrimage season (October–March) these monasteries are filled with devout Buddhists from Myanmar who come in groups for pilgrimage. The weekly direct flight by Air India, introduced in the year 1995/1996 has made the journey from Yangon to Kolkata much easier. Buddhists from Sri Lanka, Bangladesh, Thailand also come in large numbers to visit Bodhagaya, Sravasti, Vesali, Sarnath, Banaras. The Ministry of Culture of the Government of India is proactive about these initiatives. Adjacent to the main archaeological sites are the museums. Promotion of pilgrimage is a part of tourism and integral component of public diplomacy. The connectivity between Bangladesh and India, through bus service and railways has also contributed to the strengthening of the already existing Buddhist network. On certain occasions, like Kathin Chivara Dana[2] ceremony, a large number of Buddhists from Bangladesh assemble in Bodhagaya, especially to the International Meditation Centre.

Buddhism is a matter of practice among the people of Myanmar and cannot be called a "religion." There is a saying that to be a Burmese is to be a Buddhist.[3] In almost every village in Myanmar there is a monastery. People go there, pay respect to the monks, feed them, and pay homage to the Buddha. Every Myanmari wishes to visit Bodhgaya and also other places like Sarnath, Sravasti and Vesali.

Though India has lost its Buddhism in the institutional form, yet, for the Myanmar people India still enjoys a respectable status because of the origins of Buddhism here. State representatives and high officials from Myanmar always pay a visit to Bodhgaya. Visits are accompanied by donations. In the course of my visits, I was tempted to focus on the positive content of India-Myanmar relations during the colonial period. The history of the Myanmar monasteries tells us about the bonding between Bengal and eastern India with colonial Burma. Some of these aspects are highlighted here.

Early Contact

The Pagan Empire (c.849–1287) experienced destruction by the invading army of Kublai Khan in the thirteenth century. Similarly, the rise of Islam in eastern India put an unprecedented challenge to Buddhism. In the thirteenth century, the Turkic invader Bakhtiyar Khilji advanced, causing major destruction in various Buddhist establishments, including Nalanda. In the face of this extreme challenge, Buddhism went through transformation, accommodation with Vaishnavism, Saivism, even with Islam. In the thirteenth and fourteenth centuries, monasteries of eastern India turned out to be esoteric places where supernatural rites and practices were frequently heard of. At the same time, major exodus of monks was also visible in Nepal and Arakan. A large number of Hindus from Manipur and adjoining regions migrated to Upper Burma's Mandalay, where they still practice their early profession, astrology. They are often called *Ponnya.* The people of eastern India developed their own faith, but with a strong bias for Buddhism. So Buddhism did not disappear from eastern India, but had its own regional content.

We witness a resurgence of Buddhism in nineteenth-twentieth centuries. At one level, Buddhism was "rediscovered," as western scholars like Rhys Davids and Mrs. Davids, Hermann Oldenberg and Max Mûller, just to name the most eminent ones, hold. But, quite independent of western response to Buddhism and patronage, Buddhist studies generated a great deal of enthusiasm among Indian scholars too. In Bengal, the Brahma Samaj was the forerunner in promoting Buddhist values and was engaged in translating Buddhist literature, writing biographies on Buddha in Bengali language. After the founding of Pali Text Society in London in 1881, the great trio, Haraprasad Sastri, Satish Chandra Vidyabhushana and Sarat Chandra Das founded the "Buddhist Text Society" in Calcutta in 1892. The intellectual tradition got additional impetus through missions of pilgrimage originating from Buddhist countries, chiefly from Myanmar. Help from Bamar (Burman) kings and their emissaries poured in again in the fourteenth century. It continued, as we will see in the following pages. By the end of the nineteenth century, Bodhgaya had emerged as the most important Buddhist centre in India. The involvement of Myanmar royal family in the matter of Bodhgaya ended after the Third Anglo-Burmese War in 1885–86. Myanmar was eclipsed by Sri Lanka. Even then, who can ignore the contribution of U. Chandramani, U. Ottama, U. Wisara in the cause of Buddhist resurgence movement in India? The role of a number of Myanmar monks in enriching our knowledge is indicated by the fact that the

Head monk Sayadaw U Kawida of the Myanmar monastery in central Kolkata was a teacher of Myanmar texts and imbibed the *metta* and true Buddhist values.

Buddhist World of Myanmar: Importance for South Asia

Much inspiration for this work comes from my academic engagement with Myanmar and undivided Bengal, Bihar and Bangladesh. Myanmar's tradition of *Abhidhamma* and *Vinaya* observing monks was the link factor in the mainstream Theravada tradition. The Rakhine (Arakanese) model played an important role in the development of monastic order in Bengal Buddhism. At the same time, Buddhism in Myanmar has a pluralist nature, high adaptability and, a spirit of accommodation.[4] In addition, South Asian Buddhists drew inspiration from Myanmar since the country bears testimony of relic worship, directly involved with the life of the Buddha. The legend is as follows. The Buddha went to Dhanyawadi in Arakan with his five hundred disciples including the king Chandrasuriya. Thereafter, the Buddha agreed to have an image of himself, to be preserved as a symbol of his visit to Dhanyawadi. This image was to be later known as the Mahamuni image. The cult of Mahamuni appears to be extremely popular and found support not only in the minds of the Rakhine people, but also ancient people across various parts of South Asia. Pamela Gutman draws our attention to a similar legend that was popular not only in Kosambi in northwest India, but also in China. Everywhere Buddha was associated with some acts of miracle. Regarding the particular legend of Mahamuni cult, Gutman added that in China such legends became popular in the fifth century,[5] exactly the time when the Mahamuni shrine in Arakan was built. Even if we accept the supernatural powers of the Buddha as propagated by these legends, it is difficult to accept that Chinese Buddhism became the model for the dissemination and spread of Buddhism—it was royal power and influence that helped the spread and not the power of the Buddhist clergy.

India-Myanmar relations have emerged from people to people exchanges, in which the rituals associated with pilgrimage, relic worship and other spiritual activities played the central role. This started in the sixth century B.C. and continues without break till date. Such intimate contact developed also between the Buddhists of Bangladesh and Myanmar Buddhists, as is visible in the past as well as in the present. Indeed, looking at the ruins across the Rakhine State of Myanmar and Comilla Hill regions of Bangladesh, it becomes an acceptable fact that along with the Indian state of Tripura, this was a single culture-region, where Buddhism with a strong regional metaphor flourished. For the Chittagong based monks of Theravada tradition, Myanmar Buddhism, especially the Rakhine (Arakan) tradition remains the sole inspiration.

The archaeological remains of the sites of Dhanyawadi, Vesali, etc., should be considered along with similar ruins found in the Lalmai-Mainamati region.[6] The ruins in Mainamati tell the story of the Bengal kings from the Rata, Khadga, Chandra and Deva dynasties, which were the brethren of the Chandras and other rulers of ancient Arakan. There is a strong heritage of continuity of such relationships—a subject on which very little is said or written.

As late as the eighteenth-nineteenth centuries, we have excellent examples about the nature of close contact between the people of Chittagong and Arakan. Places like Ramu and Cox's Bazaar are full of beautiful Rakhine temples. The outer and inner structures of these temples resemble those that I have seen in the Khamti areas of Arunachal Pradesh. The monasteries of the Chittagong-Ramu-Cox's Bazaar area were built by the Rakhine refugees who stormed into this area on the eve of the act of annexation by the Bamar king Bodawpaya. This was in 1784 when Arakan lost its independence to the Bamar kings. Bodawpaya took away the Mahamuni image—the sole symbol of religious and political independence of Arakan. The Arakanese influx sparked off from that point of time. Within a short span of time, the Rakhine people faced another challenge. The British annexed Arakan in 1824–26 and gave refuge to the hapless people who were so cruelly oppressed by the Burmese king. This episode confirms that the Rakhine refugees were constantly being wooed by the colonial rulers, so that the old rivalry between the Rakhines and the Bamars remained alive. It thus becomes clear why the Rakhine (also known by the name "Maghs") people[7] felt so secure under the British protection. These Rakhine monasteries have in their possession relics and manuscripts, the systematic classification of which, as I understand, remains to be done. I was also further impressed by another monastery, the famous Rangkut monastery in Bangladesh. This monastery is believed to be as old as the time of King Ashoka (272–32 B.C.), who took the initiative of building 84,000 *chaityas* in various places associated with the life of Shakyamuni Buddha.

Not only is the geographical proximity between the two countries, India and Myanmar, important for this discourse. Equally significant is the religious experience that both the countries have gone through. The depth of the relation between the two countries can best be appreciated if we adequately study the details of this age old experience. The people of Myanmar and the people of India thought along the same line when it came to achievement of merit, which ultimately would lead an individual to attain the goal of *Mukti* or *Nibbana* from the circle of lives. This spiritual connectivity manifested itself in the act of pilgrimage by the common masses as well as by the royals. As a result, trade was promoted. The coastal provinces of India (Bengal, Orissa, Andhra Pradesh and Tamil Nadu) and Lower Myanmar including Arakan coast were interlinked.

Myanmar is connected by important highways that also connect China with India, Tibet and Nepal with Southeast Asia on the one hand and Central Asia on the other. Burma's state building process started in early years of Christian era when contact with Buddhists in South India was established. Lower Myanmar was actively engaged in trade which was partly dominated by the early people of modern Malaysia and Indonesia. Coastal Burma, Pegu, Martaban regions were involved in the maritime trade activities going on between the Coromandal coast of India and the Mediterranean world. Thaton, the flourishing port in ancient Lower Myanmar was dominated by the Mons, also known otherwise by the name *Talaings*. The region between Sittang and Salween rivers was known as the Mon kingdom of

Ramannadesa. Thaton (Sudhamma) was also known as *Suvaranabhumi* or Golden Land.[8] The term is widely known to Indians from classical sources. To this general terminology, we can include a number of regions around the Bay of Bengal which now belong to various countries of South Asia. All the names of major Buddhist centres of Bengal known from the inscriptional sources like Samatata, Harikela, Pattikera have their old linkages with various parts of Buddhist Myanmar.

It was from the Mons (called also Talaings) that the Mranma people borrowed their script. One however has to go back to the time of the Pyus, a Sino-Tibetan people, who, being already present in the fifth century, used a script for a Pali inscription, which had similarity with the Kadamba script used in the third century in North Canara, near Goa on the west coast. All the major archaeological sites in Myanmar bear evidence of close commercial and religious network existent between India and Myanmar. Deities of the Hindu pantheon were worshipped by the people of Myanmar just as deities of Mahayana-Tantric pantheon[9] like Avalokitesvar, Tara, etc.[10]

In view of the above, it is all too natural that many Myanmar monks (*Sayadaw*), especially from the Rakhine state (Arakan) would feel at home in India as well as in Bangladesh. They have become naturalized citizens of India. But, at the same time they maintain contacts with Myanmar. The Government of Myanmar quite often shows respect to these *Saayadaw*s for promoting *Buddhasasana* in India.

Relic Worship and Pilgrimage in the Realm of Buddhist World

To tell the story of how and why pilgrimage entered the realm of Theravada Buddhism, one has to talk of the entire narrative of the development of Buddhism from a Sangha-based organization to a mass movement with various ramifications along the line of various prevalent (non-Buddhist) ideologies and along regional roots. The monks were advised to stay in the monasteries and were expected to engage themselves in the study of the *Tripitaka* and follow Vinaya rule, etc. Travelling as such was not on the agenda. The Buddha moved to preach and to organize his Sangha. Gradually, with the emergence of an active traders' community who moved around, visits to places connected with Buddha's life came up. Such activities gained ground during King Ashoka's reign.

The basic question one asks here is what is pilgrimage? *The American Heritage* Dictionary defines pilgrimage as journey to a sacred place or shrine.[11] But, it also says that a pilgrim is the one who embarks on a quest for some end, conceived as sacred. According to *Encyclopaedia Britannica*, no single meaning can be attributed to the act of pilgrimage. Structural similarities are discernible, however, across disparate traditions of sacred travel. Pilgrimage usually entails some separation (alone or in a group) from the everyday world of home, and pilgrims may mark their new identity by wearing special clothes or abstaining from physical comforts. In the Hindu-Buddhist tradition, the thought of acquiring merit, *Punnya*, through pilgrimage is dominant. This concept is also universal in Islam as well as in Christianity. This merit or *Punnya* appears to be much desired, since this helps human beings to overcome the pain of being reborn in this world, which is full of sorrows (*dukkha*). When the Buddha was born in the sixth century B.C. in the foothills of the Himalayas, the plains from Terai-U.P. stretching up to Bihar were dotted with small kingdoms or settlements. This is called *Majjhimdesa* or Middle Kingdom in the Pali literature. From the description of Buddhist literature it becomes quite clear that large section of Buddha's followers were rich merchants, coming from well-to-do urban classes of this region.[12] They had money and contacts to build expensive edifices: temples, *stupa*s (burial mounds), guesthouses, granaries, etc. We should not neglect the fact that Gautama Buddha was a product of his own time. As much as he rejected the caste system, and the supremacy of the Brahmins in the society, he had to accommodate himself with the prevailing mood of his time. Therefore, he had to select such places for his meditation and retreat which were being visited in those days by the elites of the society: the Brahmins and wealthy merchant classes. Buddha's sojourn to Bodhgaya of Magadha for the achievement of the Enlightenment is justified, as Gaya is closely situated. In the Brahmanic tradition Gaya's importance is immense. Several temples around the place subscribe to Gaya's antiquity and its significant position in the pilgrimage tradition.[13] Vishnu worship is also noticed in the domain of Buddhism. Even Saivism influenced Buddhism, where Tantric ideas of Male-Female dichotomy played a significant role in popularizing the concept of *Upaya* (skilful means) and *Prajna* (wisdom).[14]

In the same way, Sarnath was selected by Buddha having in mind the proximity of the place to the already existing religious centre, Kashi (Varanasi). In Sarnath, Buddha gave his first sermon in a Deer Park. Thereafter, he wandered from place to place, preaching his doctrine which was based on simple realities of human life. His teachings were as follows: life is full of sorrows. The cause of this sorrow is unfulfilled desire. Therefore, desire has to be burnt down in the root. The extinction of desire (*tanha*) will bring total peace. That state of mind would finally lead to *Nibbana*. Asceticism and total withdrawal, as Buddha himself practiced by leaving behind his family and by undergoing hard penance under a native Bodhi tree (Bo tree from Simhala *bo*; English, Banyan Fig; Latin, *Ficus religiosa*) was a very difficult path indeed! For the worldly people, as well as for the ascetics, he prescribed eight paths (*astangikamarga*).[15] Within 200 years, the new faith with its core concept of *dhamma* (righteousness) spread to the remaining parts of the country, i.e. beyond the boundary of the Gangetic basin. Being aware of the great cry for remains relating to Lord Buddha, Ashoka built as many as 84,000 stupas in various parts of his kingdom. Ashoka and his *Dhamma* became an ideal paradigm for rulers of Buddhist Myanmar, as also for other countries which embraced Buddhism as the state religion.

After the Mahaparinirvana of Buddha, his followers met in various places to discuss several problems arising out of the ramifications of the faith that Buddha had preached. Such meetings are known in the Buddhist literature as "*Samgiti*." It may be relevant to note that after the third Council (*Samgiti*),

Ashoka sent his two emissaries, Sona and Uttara to *Suvarnabhumi*, in order to preach *Dhamma*. After landing in *Suvranabhumi* (Lower Myanmar), they made the people aware of sixty two wrong views and sowed the seed of *Sila* (virtue), *Samadhi* (concentration) and *Panna* (wisdom). In Myanmar, the most important and greatest Buddhist shrine, Shwedagon pagoda, is believed to be built upon the hair relic of Buddha, given to Tapussa and Bhallika, two merchants from Okkala who met the Buddha at Bodhgaya under the Bodhi tree. On their return to Okkala, with the help of Sakka, the king of gods, the hair relic was enshrined in a site on the Theinguttara hill. Here stands the gigantic pagoda! The names of the two merchants Tapussa and Bhallika are mentioned in the famous Buddhist text *Lalitavistara*.[16]

The Kushan king, Kanishka (78–101 A.D.), who ruled from his capital, Purushapura (Peshwar of modern Pakistan), spread the message of the Buddha to various parts of India and Central Asia; Mathura in the north, Amaravati in the south emerged as strong centres of Buddhism. Kanishka called the Fourth Council (*Samgiti*) at Kashmir to settle various dissensions within the Buddhist intellectual life and texts.

The next phase of progress in the Buddhist faith was experienced during the Gupta age (320– early sixth century A.D.). Hundreds of inscriptions found in various Buddhist sites (Bharhut, Sanchi, etc.) suggest emergence of ever increasing pilgrimage networks within India. The Gupta age is regarded as the golden age of Indian history, perhaps rightly so, as Buddhism and Hinduism (Saivism as well as Vaishnavism) showed their unique blending and maximum mutual accommodation with each other. India emerged as one of the most wonderful centres of cultural milieu of Asia.

Indian merchants, Indian knowledge bearers (Brahmins, in particular), Indian astrologers and ordinary adventurers found their way to various parts of what we call "Southeast Asia."[17] Various schools of Indian art, including Gupta school, Amaravati school, and Pala-Sena school, impressed the people of Myanmar considerably. An important volume by Aung Thaw, *Archaeological Sites in Burma* cites several examples of influence of such schools of art on the various culture centres which flourished simultaneously in various parts of Myanmar: Beikthano, Halin, Srikshetra, Thaton, Pagan, Tagaung, Pegu, Dagon (Yangon), Mrohaung, Ava, Sagaing, etc. There is little doubt that traders and pilgrims played an immensely significant role in this cultural intercourse. My personal experiences of these archaeological sites in Myanmar have resulted in my convictions about Myanmar's rich cultural identity that was linked with India.[18]

Impressed by the cultural renaissance that emanated from Buddhism, the Chinese pilgrim Fa hien visited India (399–414 A.D.) and furnished information on the state of Buddhism in India. He was followed by many other monks; of these, the most eminent ones were Hiuen-tsang and I-Tsing.[19] The Gupta rulers were great patrons of learning and knowledge. Narasimha Gupta Baladitya extended his support for the construction of a monastery in Nalanda, a place where later emerged the world-renowned university. Scholars from various parts of Asia poured into Nalanda, to absorb various branches of knowledge from their Indian teachers. Nalanda's fame spread far and wide, especially due to its patronage of an exclusive Indian (eastern Indian in particular) school of Tantric line. Emperor Harshavardhana of Kanauj (606–47 A.D.) was one of the last emperors of India, who, during the post-Gupta period, raised the flag of Buddhism with greatest reverence. Harsha constructed stupas, patronized Buddhist values, thus liberally supported Nalanda Mahavihara for further progress. It was during Harsha's reign that another Chinese traveller-cum-scholar, Hiuen-tsang visited Buddhist sites, shrines and centres of learning. It is usually argued that end of Harsha's rule brought about the decline of Buddhism in India. There were many reasons for this decline: firstly, the absence of rulers of such stature as that of Ashoka, Kanishka or Harsha; secondly, advance of Islam from the north and its penetration into various parts of our country; thirdly, schism that emerged within various schools of Buddhism, only a glimpse of which can be offered here within the brief scope of this paper; fourthly, decline in the centrality of royal power leading to ramifications of power. This "decline" in Buddhism in India was to the advantage of the kings of China. There seems to be an immense popularity of Buddhist shrines and Indian Buddhist classical learning during this period in China.[20]

There is evidence about close contacts between the Pala kings of Bengal–Bihar (A.D. 8–13) and the kings of Myanmar, especially the kings of the Pagan dynasty. The influence of Pala school was so prominent that Aung Thaw had to write "Not all Buddha images of Pagan period conform to Pala style."[21] A very recent study of an eminent Thai scholar

Chotima Chaturawong has examined the Pala-Pagan relation. The influence of architectural type *Bhadra* reflected in the *Sikhara* type of architecture of Pagan has been described.[22] This study along with former works done by great art historians like Ch. Duoisell, Gordon Luce and Niharranjan Ray strongly substantiate the view that there was a continuous flow of people between the heartland of Myanmar and the Bengal-Bihar region. Between these two major centres there were small city kingdoms, which contributed a lot in making this route through which pilgrims came and went, comfortable and safe. One such city kingdom was Pattikera.[23] Tantric Gods and Goddesses were extremely popular in all these places. The works of D.C. Bhattacharya and Benoytosh Bhattacharya have unravelled the religious traditions of this part of Bengal-Chittagong-Tripura region, where the Tantric Goddess Chunda enjoyed popularity or where Goddess Duragottara, enshrined in the Pattikera Monastery, was favoured.

In view of this liberal and tolerant tradition, it becomes difficult to accept the view that Mahayanists at Pagan were "outsiders." Imprints of Tantric influence evident in paintings of two Pagan temples, Payathonzu and Nandamanna, as illustrated by Dureisell and N. R Ray strongly substantiate the liberal and inviting spirit of the Myanmar Buddhists from Pagan period.[24] The Pyu and Mon base of Pagan civilization, or broadly, Myanmar civilization, carries rich heritage of interaction with the Mahayana influenced milieu of southern and eastern India. It is in the light of this, that we have to follow the architectural similarities between monasteries of Nagarjunakonda of Andhra Pradesh and Beikthano (Vishnu city) of Upper Myanmar, well illustrated by U Aung Thaw. Close connections between Nagarjunakonda and Pyu dominated Prome area has been established on the basis of archaeological evidences by Sukumar Sengupta.[25] The same author is of the opinion that *Sarvastivada-nikaya* of Myanmar, the earliest form of Sanskrit Buddhism, got inspiration from Magadha region. Therefore, we can certainly affirm that Mahayana and Tantric influence and increase of rituals promoted trade and mobility of the trader community. Various rituals (*puja*) required offerings, the demand for which increased with the emerging new world of Buddhist faith.

Another reason for liberalization of the Buddhist faith was the advent of several challenges, such as neo-Confucianism in China, Islam in the Arab world, neo-Brahmanism. Buddhism by the ninth-tenth centuries therefore had to transgress several boundaries of its traditional orthodoxy. Myanmar responded to this social call as much as India did.

The faith became diverted to more esoteric ideals and complex rituals. To understand the intricacies of such diverse forms that were inspired by Tantric beliefs originating from Hindu and Saiva traditions one has to appreciate the social compulsions and political environment in India from the ninth century onwards. On the one hand, permissiveness was indulged in the domain of orthodoxy, on the other hand, various *yana*-s (paths) were discovered to attain Buddhahood. Amidst all these, the dynamics of worshiping Buddha relics went on. In the case of Myanmar, the major races, the Burmans, the Shans and the Mons were all Buddhists and therefore relation with India continued. Most importantly, the Rakhine state (Arakan), the oldest of all the states of Myanmar, offered passage to enter the Indian sub-continent through Chittagong of present Bangladesh. The word "Chittagong" itself has been derived from "Chaityagrama", the village of Chaityas. Due to their ritual and academic potentiality, the importance of Bodhgaya-Nalanda area enhanced immensely. To face the various challenges, the Pagan kings of Myanmar became keen to form an alliance with Bengal. At this point of time, the old Arakan-Chittagong route regained its importance. The Pagan king Kyanzittha (A.D. 1084–1113) was so keen to tie a knot with Bengal that he married a Bengali lady, named Abeyadana. A series of paintings from Abeyadana temple built by Kyanzittha bear influences of Brahmanism, Mahayanism as well as Theravada Buddhism.[26]

There are further examples of spread of Mahamuni cult in various directions beyond the boundary of Arakan. The temple of Madhav at Hajo in Kamrupa district of Assam is one such example.[27] It is said that originally the temple was a Buddhist shrine, only to become a place of worship for the Hindus. Interestingly, the temple deity is known as Mahamuni. Now, it is a place of pilgrimage for Hindus and Buddhists alike.

In order to examine social and economic forces that were at work, one needs to take a look at the inner clashes that surfaced, apparently around rather insignificant issues, but, in reality, there might have been major factors causing such dissensions and divisions. The development of Buddhism with its various branches has to be seen in the context of the individual history of the concerned regions in which they developed. Without going into the details of these regional variations of Buddhism, for the time being, we can concentrate on general divisions within the faith.[28] For example, the progressive *Mahasanghika* and the conservative *Sthaviravada* schools were almost at loggerheads. The Mahayana school appeared from the fold of the Mahasanghikas. The Mahayana itself gave birth to several branches, such as *Sahajayna*, *Mantrayana*, *Vajrayana* and *Kalacakrayana*. According to Biswanath Banerjee, Kalacakra system showed maximum accommodation with the Hindu Gods and Goddesses.[29] It went to such an extent that it became difficult to draw a line between Buddhist Tantra and Hindu Tantrashastra. Such amalgamation and accommodation between Hinduism and Buddhism made pilgrimage most interesting an experience for the common masses. Kalacakrayana was quite firmly established in Tibet. But liberal trend within Mahayana Buddhism in particular and Buddhism generally was not only visible in India and Tibet but also in Nepal and Myanmar.

Coming to the subject of history of modern India and the role of persons and institutions contributing to the resurgence of Buddhism, the name of a South Asian monk Anagarika Dharmapala, is held in high esteem. He was inspired by Edwin Arnold, author of *Light of Asia*, who stressed upon the urgent need to renovate and reconstruct the greatest Buddhist temple, the Mahabodhi temple at Bodhgaya. Anagarika Dharmapala established the Mahabodhi Society in Colombo in 1891 and, later, a branch of it, in Calcutta in 1892. The names of his two mentors, Col. Olcott and Mrs. Foster, deserve mention;

the first one took him to various places in British Burma and the second one donated a handsome amount of money for the promotion of Dharmapala's mission. According to Ananda Guruge, Mahabodhi Society received liberal donations from the Buddhists of Myanmar (British Burma), particularly from Arakan, for building guesthouses in Bodhgaya and Sarnath.[30] It is through Dharmapala and Olcott that the great Myanmar monk of Arakanese origin, U. Chandramani made the first contact with India. The meeting place between the three was Akyab (modern Sittwe), the capital of Arakan.

The area Gaya-Bodhgaya remained all through a centre of attention for the Myanmar kings. In 1820, king Bodawpaya (1782–1819) of Alaungpaya dynasty dispatched an emissary to Bodhgaya with a map to find out the exact location of the Mahabodhi tree. The mission was also aimed at locating the spot of the actual temple. The mission failed, apparently due to physical inaccessibility of the area. The area was full of jungles. Therefore, the emissary went back to Mandalay. The next emissary was sent by the next king Bagyidaw of the same dynasty. This emissary could locate the spot of the Mahabodhi tree. In 1833, the Myanmar emissary discovered an inscription in Myanmar script written in Pali language. This inscription tells us the long and untold story of the Mahabodhi temple.[31]

This relation between Bodhgaya and the Myanmar kings of Alaungpaya dynasty made further progress during the time of the king Mindon Min (1853–78). There is significant literature on Mindon Min's religious policies, aiming at Buddhist reform, purification process and resurgence. Mindon

Min called the Fifth Buddhist synod in the capital, Mandalay. Mindon paid attention to various aspects. On the one hand he built a guest house in Bodhgaya for the pilgrims coming from his country (1784), on the other hand, he was equally mindful in promoting Buddhist morale along the Chittagong frontier. Therefore, we see that the monk Sangharaja Saramedha was invited to his capital. Sangharaja Saramedha's name is still remembered with deepest reverence by the Bengali Buddhists, especially the Chakmas. It was this great monk who took initiative to purify the Buddhist order in the Chittagong Hill Tracts at a point of time when Buddhism was challenged by impure corrupt practices.[32] King Mindon Min recognized the works of Saramedha and the Sangharaja Nikaya (Sangharaja order) as the legitimate order of the Buddhist Sangha. The Arakanese Buddhist heritage was also got rejuvenated by the introduction of *Mahamuni Mela* by the Chakma queen Rani Kalindi. This close contact between Chittagong and Arakan still exists.

Shrines, Archaeological Sites and Myanmar Monasteries in Bihar, Uttar Pradesh and Lumbini

In this section, I try to describe the shrines, monasteries and archaeological sites in an order that matches with the introductory discussion at the outset. The sequence is as follows: Lumbini (Buddha's birthplace), Sravasti, Kushinagar, Vesali, Rajgriha, Bodhgaya, Varanasi, Sarnath, Pataliputra, Nalanda and Nava Nalanda. As is known to us, in and around 1860s, Sir A. Cunnigham discovered a number of shrines in all these places. But, after him, various other officials continued the task in collaboration with their Indian counterparts. The eminent Buddhist scholar Rajendralal Mitra extended his assistance to Sir Cunningham in the excavation of Bodhgaya temple and surroundings. The news of discoveries of such ruins inspired Myanmar people even in those days, to come to India, to offer donation towards maintenance of the sites. For example, in 1927, the main stupa of Kushinagar was completely restored thanks to the generous donation of U Po Kyu and U Po Hlaing of Myanmar.[33] In *Dikkhanikaya* of *Mahaparinibbana Sutta*, Buddha told his disciple Ananda that there would be four major places of pilgrimage. These were Lumbini, Bodhgaya, Sarnath and Kushinagar. Apart from Buddhist and Pali studies, what further enriched the movement of Bengal renaissance was the archaeological excavations that have been made in the country.

Lumbini

Lumbinī is located in the Rupamdehi district of Nepal, in the Indian border. In the garden of Lumbini, under the shadow of a Shal tree (*Shorea robusta*), mother Maya, wife of king Suddhadhana, gave birth to Siddhartha Gautama. Lumbini is in the foothills of the Himalayas, 25 km east of the municipality of Kapilavastu. Suddhadhana was the king of Kapilavastu, the small kingdom in the foothills of the Himalaya, where the Buddha is said to have lived till the age of 29. The Buddha lived between roughly 563 and 483 BCE. Lumbini is one of four magnets for pilgrimage that sprang up in places pivotal to the life of the Buddha. Lumbini has a number of temples, including the Mayadevi temple and others under construction. There are the remains of Kapilvastu palace as well. Also there is the *Puskarini* or Holy Pond where the Buddha's mother took the ritual dip prior to his birth and where he, too, had his first bath.

Entering Lumbini, any one would have the feel of pilgrimage. It had already become a place of pilgrimage during Emperor Ashoka's time. Ashoka himself visited the place after completion of twenty years of his ascendance on the throne of Magadha. At Lumbini, there is an inscription by Ashoka in Brahmi script and in Prakrit language.

This Myanmar Buddhist monastery is the only monastery which is maintained and run by the Government of Myanmar. The guesthouse and the adjoining garden are also quite impressive. It was U Thant, the former General Secretary of United Nations, and a very close friend of U Nu, who proposed as early as in 1970s to start such a guesthouse-cum-monastery in this Himalayan kingdom. After all, with Nepal, Myanmar shares a long history of religious and cultural relations. Nepal has a unique history of Hindu-Buddhist amalgamation and syncretic ideas. Nepal, like India and Myanmar, has absorbed and assimilated various ideas through its own power of integration. In many ways, it shares a common history with eastern India, especially Bengal. To properly estimate the nature of the religion of Nepal, one has to study various branches of Mahayana (especially Vajrayana School) Buddhism. In one of my earlier writings on the Ari cult of Pagan, I have argued for existence of various popular cults related to a tradition of a common Mahayana worship in various parts of Nepal, Tibet, Bengal and Myanmar. Buddhism as practiced by the Tibetans bears distinct similarities with the Hindu-Buddhist tradition of Nepal. Every year in the month of September two thousand Tibetan Lamas assemble in Lumbini to perform various Pujas while praying for world peace.[34]

Sravasti

Śrāvastī or Sāvatthī, a city of ancient India, was one of the six largest cities and most affluent city-kingdoms (*Mahajanapadas*) in India during Gautama Buddha's life time. The city was located in the fertile Gangetic plains, located about 120 km north of Lucknow. It belongs to the present day Gonda district of U.P. Sravasti is much esteemed a place in the domain of Buddhist pilgrimage. Numerous references have been found in *Ramayana*, *Mahabharata*, *Puranas* and Buddhist literatures on the kingdom of Kosala, in which Sravasti is situated. Sravasti has been mentioned by Fa Hien and Hiuen-tsang in their respective accounts. The ruins in Sravasti, called Sahet Mahet, were identified by Sir A. Cunnigham in 1863. Subsequently the excavations were carried forth by Vogel, Marshall and Daya Ram Sahni in the years 1907–08, 1910–11.

The name of Sudatta or Anathapindika (feeder of deserted children) is closely associated with Sravasti. Jetavana monastery was a famous monastery close to Sravasti. It was the second monastery donated to Buddha, after the Veluvana in Rajagriha. Jeta, son of king Prosenjit, and Sudatta, were deeply impressed by Buddha's doctrines. They offered him land and resources to build *viharas* in Sravasti. Majority of the sermons recorded in the *Tripitaka* were delivered while Buddha was spending his time in Jetavan Vihara. For example, out of 350 rules of discipline for monks, 297 rules were prescribed by Buddha while he was staying in Jetavan Vihara. According to *Mahavastu*, the Buddha performed miracles (known as twin miracles) and impressed thousands of his disciples.[35] We have already mentioned the impact of such miraculous incidents about the people of Asia, including China. This and other intensive interactions with his followers were possible since Buddha spent as many as 45 rainy seasons in Sravasti only. King Ashoka visited Sravasti and built two pillars on the eastern gate of Jetavahana. Ashoka also built a temple here. Thus, this place, like any other place where king Ashoka's name is associated, deserves a special attention from Myanmar pilgrims. Also pilgrims from Sri Lanka come here in great numbers.

Equally impressive appears to be the two mounds — called Kuccha Kuthi and Pukka Kuthi. The latter mound was identified by Cunnigham as the Angulimalastupa. In the history of India-Myanmar relations, Sravasti has a special role to play. Sravasti successfully bears the tradition of building of Myanmar guesthouses for Myanmar pilgrims, which started from the time of Mindon Min (?–1878). There is an old guesthouse-cum-monastery, built during 1920s, for the accommodation of Myanmar (Burmese) pilgrims. This monastery-cum-guesthouse has a very impressive architectural style. It was built during 1920s with the rich donation of Myanmar families from what was then colonial Burma. U. Chandramani inspired the construction of such an establishment in view of the rising number of pilgrims pouring in from Myanmar. The resident monk Ven. U. Awbatha from the newly built Sravasti monastery offered me accommodation in the new monastery. Yet, as I witnessed, every day Sayadaw U. Awbatha went to the old monastery and performed all his duties as the Head Monk.

Kushinagar

Kushinagar, Kusinagar or Kusinara is a town in the district Kushinagar of U.P. It is located to the Indian side near the border of India and Nepal. Kushinagar is the place where Shakyamuni Buddha breathed his last. Buddha passed away at the age of 80 in the year 545 B.C., while this great soul was residing in the *Sal* forest of the king of the Mallas. Kushinagar is famous for the Mahaparinirvana temple and the large reclining Buddha image. In the fifth century A.D., a wealthy merchant, obviously a devout, from Mathura brought the image to Kushinagara. In the year 1876, archaeologist Carlleyle discovered the image by excavating to a depth of 10 feet. From the excavation, other discoveries including human skeletons came into light. This signifies that the place was destroyed by outsiders. Most interesting for me remains the 75 feet high stupa, which carries the memory of Buddha's last days in Kushinagar. In 1910, during the excavation, the stupa was only 24 feet. But, Hiuen-tsang described the stupa as 200 feet high. A Myanmari couple generously donated money for the restoration of the main stupa. In 1956, while

India was observing the 2500 (two thousand five hundred) years of Lord Buddha's Mahaparinirvana, the stupa was again renovated.

With the very name Kushinagar, U. Chandramuni's name is inevitably linked. But, we should also remember the name of Mahavir, a nephew of one Babu Kunwar Singh, a bold soldier of India's First War of Independence, in 1857. Mahavir, being a Hindu was attracted to Buddhism. He went to Sri Lanka and came back full of inspiration to promote *Buddhasasana* in India. He repaired the main temple and started the *Dharmasala* (guesthouse) in 1901. The cost of the construction of the guesthouse, however, was borne by a devout Buddhist from Arakan with the name Khezari Babu.[36]

The notable Arakanese monk U. Chandramani played the most constructive role in bringing to the memory of the Indian people the age old relation between Myanmar and India. For fulfilling this mission he thought that the first step should be to renovate the edifices which carry the memory of this relation. Therefore, he was engaged in renovating the pilgrim houses and monasteries in Sravasti, Kushinagar, and as we will later see, also in Sarnath. It is no wonder that Dr. B.R. Ambedkar turned to this eminent monk when the former decided to embrace Buddhism. There is a small temple within the premises of Kushinara monastery, quite legitimately named as "Dikshabhumi". This small temple carries the memory of the meeting of the guru, U. Chandramuni and his *sishya*, Dr. B.R. Ambedkar. Ambedkar's contact with Myanmar progressed further, and continued up to his demise.

He was one of the members of the Indian delegation that went to attend the fifth Buddhist Council in Yangon (Rangoon) in the year 1956. This great soul of India, seen by neo Buddhists as one of the Avataras of Buddha, visited Myanmar at least twice.

Dr. Ambedkar's guru Ven. U. Chandramani established schools and hospitals in various parts of India, where Buddhist shrines are situated. Of course Kushinagar remained his centre of activities. Further, Chandramani dedicated himself to learning Sanskrit, Hindi and other Indian languages. Seth Jugal Kishor Birla, renowned philanthropist, stood by his side in all his noble activities. In the premises of the monastery of Kushinagar, there is a small charitable hospital in the name of U. Chandrmuni. As in other Myanmar monasteries, here too, there is a big replica of the Shwedagon Pagoda. Seth Jugal Kishor Birla was the one who took the financial responsibility of Tagore's visit to Myanmar in 1924.[37]

Sayadaw (Guruji) Ven. Jnaneswar, the head monk of the Kushinagar Myanmar monastery, is a direct pupil of U. Chandramani. Carrying the legacy of that great monk, Jnaneswar is involved in various social welfare activities, not only in Kushinagar, but in various parts of India, and even beyond India. Following the footsteps of his Guru U Chandramanani, Ven. Jnaneswar has also been active in the development of Kushinagar from an "unknown" village to a moderate town. In the year 2007, Ven. Jnaneswar was awarded the title of "Agga Maha Pandita Sadhhamma Jyotika Dhaja" by the Government of Myanmar. The monastery brings out a journal with the title *Nibban Bodhi*.

Vesali

The city of Vaishali or Vesali (Pali), Basarh in the Muzaffarpur district of Bihar, is 2-3 hours drive from Patna, the old Pataliputra. It was the capital city of the Licchavi clan, one of world's first democratic republics, in the Vajjian Confederacy (Vrijji) Mahajanapada, around the sixth century BC.[38] In the Valmiki *Ramayana* and in *Puranas*, this city has been mentioned as Vishalpuri, which was founded by king Vishal of Ishkkhu dynasty. Due to its association with Rama of *Ramayana*, Jaina Tirthankar Mahavira and other personalities, this place enjoys a high position in the Indian tradition in general. The 24th prophet of the Jainas, Mahavira was born in Vesali. The monolithic pillar Kolhua (Vesali) created by the king Ashoka is very impressive.

No wonder, Buddha was much impressed by the rich heritage of this place. Therefore, he established a "Bhikkhu Sangha" here with his idea of republican model. More important is the fact that it was a place where Lord Buddha declared the inauguration of Bhikkhuni Sangha[39] in honour of his foster mother (*Dhatrimata*). Buddha's special love for Vesali brought him back to the place time and again. While he was engaged in preaching and enlightening the people, he also foresaw that his days for *Mahaprinibbana* were approaching. Buddha preached his last sermon before his death in 483 BC. On one hundred years of Buddha's Mahaparinibbana, in 383 BC, the Second Buddhist Council was convened here by King Kalasoka, making it an important place of pilgrimage in Jain and Buddhist religions.[40]

The importance of Vesali in the world of Buddhism can be ascertained by the fact that in the kingdom of Arakan, the Rakhine state of Myanmar, the small city kingdom was named after the same name, Vesali.[41] After the passing away of Buddha his mortal corporeal remains were in great demand. Buddha's body was claimed by all those he came into contact. It was decided then to divide the corporeal remains into eight parts. The Licchavis got their share too.

Rajagriha

Rajgir (Sanskrit, Rājagṛha; Pali, Rājagaha, "house of the king" or "royal house") is a city and a notified area in Nalanda district of Bihar. Rajagriha was the capital of one of the most powerful empires of Asia, the Magadha empire and later Mauryan empire. Its date of origin is unknown, although ceramics dating to about 1000 BC have been found in the city. Rajagriha is around 100 km from both Patna and Mokameh. It is located in a green valley surrounded by rocky hills. This place has a special appeal to devout Buddhists, no matter from where they come from. Buddha preached his doctrine in Rajagriha after His enlightenment. One of Buddha's disciples from the Magadha empire was Emperor Bimbisara. Ajatsatru's aggressive opposition to the preaching of Buddha caused the imprisonment of his father, Bimbisara.

Rajagriha's special importance lies in its antiquity as a place of early monk-settlements called *avasas* and *aramas*.[42] These were in great need as the members of the Sangha wanted to take rest, or needed little privacy. The Veluvanarama was the first gift of *arama* offered to the Buddha and his Sangha by Emperor Bimbisara. The Jivikarama is yet another *arama* at Rajgirha. This place of retreat was a gift from the renowned physician Jivika. It is no wonder, therefore, that the Myanmar people, who are in contact with the Indian people over thousands of years would love to have a guesthouse and monastery in Rajagriha, the oldest place of *aramas* and *avasas*. The Myanmar monastery in Rajagriha has two parts. The first building stands from the 1920s. The architectural decoration bears similarities with the Myanmar monastery of Sravasti. The new building houses the pilgrims from Myanmar. It has a library, which is named after Aung San, the father of the Myanmar Nation.

Bodhgaya

It is the main temple, the Mahabodhi temple and the Bodhi tree that has attracted Buddhist devotees from across the world. In 2002, the Mahabodhi Temple has been declared as a World Heritage Site by UNESCO.

Already in the second half of the thirteenth century Myanmar people showed keen interest to improve the condition of the Mahabodhi temple. The Myanmar king Mindon Min, with the permission of the Government of British India started the restoration work on the Mahabodhi temple.[43] The breaking off of the Third Anglo-Burmese War (1885–86) brought visible changes in the British policy towards Myanmar kings and their relation with India's holy places. As is known to us, there was a battle between the *Mahantas* and Anagarika Dharmapala over the possession of the Mahabodhi temple. It was found out that without the involvement of U. Chandramani, it became difficult for Anagarika Dharmapala to continue the battle to completely regain the sanctity of Bodhgaya. U. Chandramani's involvement was badly needed, who took him to the interned king Thibaw, staying at Ratnagiri.

The Myanmar monastery called "Burmese Vihar, Bodhagaya" which was most probably built during 1930s, has quite a large campus with Ordination Hall, Prayer Hall, a garden and a guest house. While going through the monasteries in Bodhgaya, I came across, besides Myanmar pilgrims, also a large number of pilgrims from various other countries, Sri Lanka, Thailand, Bangladesh, for example. Hindus and neo-Buddhists from Maharashtra come in large number to pay homage to the Buddha in his place of Enlightenment.

Myanmar is active in spreading Buddha *sasana* in India. Rastrapala Mahathera, founder of the International Meditation Centre Boddhgaya is one of them. He was awarded the title "Agga Mahasadhhamajotikadhwaja" by the Government of Myanmar. Even earlier, Ven. Rastrapala Mahathera was a guest of Myanmar (then called Union of Burma) Government during the time 1954-1956 when the Sixth Buddhist Council was held at Yangon. He must have met Dr. Ambedkar in Yangon, when the latter visited the region as one of the members of the Indian delegation.

Varanasi

Varanasi (Sanskrit, *Vārānasī*), also commonly known as Benares or Kashi, is a city situated on the banks of the river

Ganges in U.P. It is the holiest place for the Hindus across the world. According to Hindu Cosmology, Varanasi is the centre of earth. Jains also regard it as a holy place. The city of Varanasi is one of the oldest and continuously inhabited cities, known to the world. Varanasi is also known to the Buddhists of the world, as it is mentioned repeatedly in the Buddhist literatures (*Jatakas* and *Avadanas*) due to its association of Buddha and his followers.

In the city of Varanasi, there is an important Myanmar temple in Sigra area, lying right on the main road. This Sigra Vihar was also started by U. Chandramani around the year 1920. He deputed Ven. U. Kittima to look after the construction. U Kittima, a very learned monk, later became the Second Chief Resident Monk of Sarnath Myanmar monastery. He passed away in 1987. There is yet another institution, called Myanmar Buddhist Cultural Centre. I saw Myanmar pilgrims in large numbers coming to this place.

Sarnath

Sarnath is located 13 kilometres north-east of Varanasi in U.P. It is situated in the Deer Park where Buddha first taught His *Dhamma* to five of his closest disciples. In Sarnath, the Dhammachakka Vihara Migadawon Myanmar Temple bears a rich legacy of an intensive interaction between Myanmar pilgrims and Indian people. Here too I could personally pay respect to the Chief Resident Monk Ven. U Wannadhaza. He was also born in Arakan, but since many years has been living in Sarnath. U. Chandramani started this vihara in the year 1905. This monastery in the place of Buddhas's first sermon has grown steadily, attracting patronage with liberal donation from Myanmar people.[44]

Pataliputra

Pātaliputra or modern-day Patna was originally built by Ajatashatru in 490 BC as a small fort (Pātaligrama) near the river Ganges, and, later, made the capital of one of the ancient Mahajanapadas, the kingdom of Magadha. The city witnessed the rise and fall of mighty empires of the Mauryas and the Guptas. Pataliputra or modern-day Patna is associated with the two most ancient religions of the world, namely, Buddhism and Jainism. It is from this capital of his kingdom that Emperor Ashoka sent his peace missions to Sri Lanka, and later to other places, including to *Suvannabhumi* (Lower Myanmar). Under Ashoka's patronage the third Synod was also held in Pataliputra. Realizing the importance of this place for the Myanmar people, an eminent monk with the name Thirizeya established a monastery cum guesthouse in the Rajendra Nagar area of Patna.[45] The monastery itself was inaugurated as late as 1988-1989. But the ground work started as early as 1954 when Ven. Thirizeya started "Pataliputra Association" in Yangon (Rangoon). In this monastery (Kyaung) of Rajendra Nagar, I met a number of pilgrims from Myanmar, some interesting people of Myanmar and a few monk scholars, who are staying in the monastery.

Nalanda

Nālandā is an old city located about 89 km southeast of Patna,

Bihar. It was an ancient city of higher learning and houses the relics of the ancient Nalanda University. Nalanda though might have been founded earlier, started to function from the time of the Guptas. However, there is a view that king Ashoka in the third century B.C. presented offering to the Chaitya at Nalanda, erected in memory of the great disciple of Buddha, Sariputta.[46] In the nineteenth century, Buchanon Hamilton, the famous British traveller located the place where a number of Hindu and Buddhist objects lay scattered. Later, Sir A. Cunnigham identified the place with ancient Nalanda. During 1915–16, through extensive restoration by the Archaeological Survey of India, the place acquired its present form. From the fifth century up to the twelfth century, Nalanda stood with all its glory as the supreme centre of learning in Asia, attracting a large number of scholars from China, Korea, Indonesia, Malaysia and other countries. Eminent teachers like Silabhadra, Santarakshita and Atisa Dipankar taught various branches of Indian knowledge, Buddhism in particular at this University.

Concluding Remarks

The ritual of worshipping shrines (stupas, relics, etc.) and paying homage to Lord Buddha is not an isolated act. The people of Myanmar looked at India with great enthusiasm whenever new excavations unearthing the Buddhist past of India were brought to light. This happened throughout history, perhaps from the time of Lord Buddha. Promotion of Pali and Buddhist studies at the Universities of Calcutta and Visva

Bharati (Santiniketan) started from the early years of the twentieth century. This attracted the attention of the Myanmar people, monks, students and political leaders alike.

In various parts of India too, there were Buddhist resurgence movements, stories of which reached the shore of British Burma. The works and missions of other great Buddhists from India also left a lasting impression on Myanmar people. They are Ven. Bodhananda, Rahul Sankritayana, Ven. Jagdish Kashyap, Dharmananda Kosambi, Ananda Kausalyayan—just to name a few. It is no wonder therefore that a large number of monk scholars come to various universities of India till this day to study Sanskrit, Pali and Buddhism. To my knowledge, Navanalanda Mahavihar has the largest number of monk scholars. The Magadha University of Gaya has also a number of students from Myanmar, a fact that I experienced during my field trip to Bodhgaya and Nalanda.

During colonial rule, especially during 1920s and 1930s, the Indian National Congress gave a suitable platform to a number of Myanmar monks and laymen to remain in contact with the cultural and political life of India. Buddhism and a feeling of shared past was the inspiring spirit behind this relation. Bengal in those days was very closely associated with this cultural movement, and Rabindranath Tagore was in the centre of this renaissance. Tagore's three visits to Myanmar (1916, 1924 and 1927) were reflections of his quest for understanding the essence of this great people. He knew that to achieve that one has to take refuge under the cool shadow of the Shwedagon. He found such a grand peace that he did not feel like leaving the place at all. Also Mahatma Gandhi's close friendship with the *Pongyis* (monks) speaks for his deep understanding of Myanmar Buddhism.

We ought to remember that Greater India Society was founded in this city only. In modern India, one of the first Viharas was constructed in Bengal in 1920, the magnificent Dharmarajika Chaitya at the Mahabodhi Society. The sacred relics of Lord Buddha, unearthed during an excavation at Bhattiprolu in the region of South India, were brought to Calcutta. Much to the enthusiasm of the people of Bengal the relics were enshrined in the Dharmarajika Vihara. It is in the context of this long tradition of mutual respect and recognition that one has to understand the symbolic gift, a sapling from the Bodhi tree, of the first President of the Republic of India, Dr. Rajendra Prasad, to the people of independent Myanmar on the occasion of the festivities of independence celebration on 4January 1948.

Under the initiative of Jawaharlal Nehru, in collaboration with the Governor of West Bengal Kailash Nath Katju and Shyamaprasad Mukherjee, General Secretary of the Mahabodhi Society the urn of Shariputta and Maudgalyayan was brought to the Mahabodhi Society of Kolkata (Calcutta) from Sanchi. Prior to that, it was brought ceremonially to Sanchi from London in the presence of Prime Minister U Nu, Home Minsiter of Sri Lanka and a number of top ranking statesmen from India.[47] A part of the urn later was sent to Yangon, to the "World peace Pagoda" (Kaba Aye) during the sixth Buddhist Council which was held in during 1954–56. The legendary friendship (*metta*) between the two Prime

Ministers, U Nu of Myanmar and Jawaharlal Nehru of India was based on Buddhist values of mutual respect. A large number of Buddhist shrines and excavated sites covered by my above description went through renovation, extension and reconstruction during 1950s and 1960s under direct patronage of Jawaharlal Nehru. But, it is also equally true that the people of India in those days felt an inner urge to be reconnected with countries like Sri Lanka, Myanmar and Thailand, with which they share a common heritage. We should not forget that Dr. B.R. Ambedkar was deeply impressed by this *Zeitgeist*, and quite naturally for his conversion to Buddhism he selected U. Chandramani as his guru. As has been indicated above, a large number of monks from Myanmar came to India also during 1950s. Those monks can be regarded as true successors of great monks like U. Ottama and U. Wisara, in whose vision there was no distinction between India and Myanmar so far the cultural identity of the people is concerned.

There exists not only a geographical proximity between India and Myanmar, but also a close cultural kinship between the two. The two regions seem to me a seamless tapestry representing intermingling of various races and religious beliefs, but the inner strength of which came from the regions' age old adherence to Buddhism.

Acknowledgement

Following the usual Buddhist norm of paying respect, let me first express my deep sense of gratitude and indebtedness to the following respected monks for their active support and valuable inspiration:

Ven. Dr. U. Nandabatha (Barasat, Kolkata), Ven. Dr. Varasambodhi Thera (Bodhgaya), Ven. U Awbatha (Sravasti), Agga Maha Pandita Sadhhamma Jyotika Dhaja Ven. Jnaneswar (Kushinagar), Ven. Sangha bodhi (Bodhgaya) Ven. U Wannadhaza (Sarnath),

To my teacher, who taught me Buddhism, Pali and Prakrit, Professor Biswanath Banerjee, former Professor and Head of the Department of Sanskrit, Pali and Prakrit, Visva Bharati University, Santiniketan and currently President of the Asiatic Society, Kolkata, I express my heartfelt gratitude. For my field trip and related works in connection with this project I received valuable help from the following scholars: Professor Dr. Suranjan Das, Vice-Chancellor, University of Calcutta, Professor Lipi Ghosh, Director, Centre for South & Southeast Asian Studies and Professor, Department of South & Southeast Asian Studies, Professor Bhaskar Chakrabarti, Director, Centre for Studies in Social Sciences and Humanities and Centenary Professor, Department of History, University of Calcutta. To Dr. Suchandana Chatterjee, Fellow, Maulana Abul Kalam Azad Institute of Asian Studies, Kolkata I feel extremely thankful for her keen interest to have me as one of the contributors in this volume. As always, for all my works on Myanmar, for this work too, I received kind cooperation from the Consulate General of the Republic of the Union of Myanmar for which I remain indebted. I take this opportunity to thank all the individuals, monks or laymen, institutions and monasteries for their inspiration.

Notes and References

1. Swapna Bhattacharya, *India and Myanmar: People, Pilgrimage, Histories and the Present,* Occasional paper III (Kolkata: Centre for South & Southeast Asian Studies, University of Calcutta 2010).
2. In all the Buddhist monasteries this ceremony is observed with great enthusiasm.
3. Heinz Bechert, "To be a Burmese is to be a Buddhist: Buddhism in Burma," in *The World of Buddhism*, Heinz Bechert and Richard Gombrich (eds.) (London: Thames and Hudson 1993).

4. Swapna Bhattacharya, "History of Buddhism in Myanmar: Interpretation from Indian Perspective," *Journal of the Asiatic Society of Bengal* 47, no. 4 (2005): 65–81; Nyanissara Mahathera, "Buddhism in Myanmar," in Hemendu Bikash Chowdhury (ed.), *Jagajjyoti (1908-2008)*, Centenary Volume (Kolkata: Bauddha Dharmankur Sabha 2009).
5. Pamela Gutmann, *Burma's Lost Kingdoms, Splendours of Arakan* (Bangkok: Orchid Press 2001), 29.
6. Barrie M. Morrison, *Lalmai, a Cultural Centre of Early Bengal: An Archaeological Report and Historical Analysis* (Seattle: University of Washington Press 1974). For Buddhism in Bengal see Puspa Niyogi, *Buddhism in Ancient Bengal* (Calcutta: Jijnasa 1980).
7. Abdul Mabud Khan, *The Maghs: A Buddhist Community in Bangladesh* (Dhaka: The University Press 1999).
8. In my understanding, the epithet *Sonar Bangla* (Golden Bengal) could be indicative of the possibility that eastern Bengal was included in the domain of *Suvarnabhumi*.
9. Niharranjan Ray, *Sanskrit Buddhism in Burma* (Bangkok: Orchid Press 2002); Niharranjan Ray, *Brahmanical Gods in Burma* (Bangkok: Orchid Press 2001).
10. It is interesting to mention in this context the Tibetan monk Taranath mentioned in his *history of Buddhism* that Mahayana Buddhism flourished in the *Kokibhumi* (land of the Kokis) under which he included Pugan (Pagan empire), Rakhan (Arakan) and Hamsavati (Pegu, the seat of the Mons). See Niharranjan Ray, *Sanskrit Buddhism in Burma*, 93 ff.
11. Niels Gutschow, "Pilgrimage and Space: Case Studies from Bhakatpur, Muktinath and Varanasi," in *Pilgrimage: Sacred Landscapes and Self-organised Complexity*, John Mc Kim Malville and Baidyanath Saraswati (eds.) (Indira Gandhi Centre for the arts, New Delhi: D.K. Printworld P. Ltd. 1999), 59.
12. Richard Gombrich, *Theravada Buddhism: A Social History of Ancient Benares to Modern Colombo* (London: Routledge 1988), 57. For Buddhist centres and map on spread of Buddhism see P. Nag (ed.), *Cultural Heritage Atlas of India*, NATMO (National

Atlas & Thematic Mapping Organization) Department of Science & Technology, Government of India, Kolkata 2007, 21–24.

13. Rana P.B. Singh, John Mc Kim Malville, Anne L. Marshall, "Death and Transformation at Gaya: Pilgrimage, Ancestors and the Sun," in Malville and Saraswati (eds.), *Pilgrimage*, 103.
14. Sashi Bhusan Dasgupta, *Obscure Religious Cult* (Calcutta: Firma K.L. 1969), 29.
15. The eightfold path is the combination of: Right view, Right Intension, Right Speech, Right Action, Right Livelihood, Right Effort, Right Mindfulness, Right Concentration.
16. Kashmir played an immensely important role in the spread of Buddhism in central Asia and China. According to P.C. Bagchi Kashmir was an important centre of Sarvastivada sect of the Mahayana school. The Kushan emperors contributed a lot to the prosperity of Buddhist tradition in Kashmir. It is interesting that Kumarajiva, the great Buddhist scholar, was brought from Kuci to Kashmir for higher education in the Buddhist lore. For further details on Kashmir Buddhism and spread of Buddhism in China, see P.C. Bagchi, *India and China: A Thousand Years of Cultural Relations* (Calcutta: Sarswat Library 1981), 45–53. On the maritime route, the Srivijaya empire of Indonesia played a similar role in connecting China with eastern India, Bengal in particular.
17. The nomenclature "Southeast Asia" is a modern invention. It was during the World War II when the word "Southeast Asia" was first used. Lord Mountbetten started the Southeast Asia Command to fight the Japanese on the soil of Burma.
18. Swapna Bhattacharya, "My Journey through Myanmar: Culture, People and History," *Asia Annual*, H.S. Vasudevan (editor in chief), Kaushik Bandyopadhyaya (Issue Editor) (2008): 349–58.
19. Ravindra Panth (ed.), *India's Perception through Chinese Travellers* (Nalanda: Nava Nalanda Mahavihara 2007).
20. Tansen Sen, *Buddhism, Diplomacy and Trade: The Realignment of Sino-Indian Relations 600-1400* (Honolulu: University of Hawaii Press 2003), chapter 2. For Buddhism in China see also Tan Chung, "Relations between the Indian and Chinese Civilizations," in *India*

and Asia: P.C. Bagchi Centenary Volume, B.N. Mukherjee (ed.) (Kolkata: Progressive Publishers 2009), 75–91.

21. Aung Thaw, *Historical Sites in Burma* (Ministry of Union Culture, Government of Union of Burma 1978), 83, 112.
22. Chotima Chaturawong, *Art and Architecture of Pagan in Burma and Eastern India under Pala-Sena*, Occasional Paper II, 2009–2012 (Kolkata: Centre for South & Southeast Asian Studies, University of Calcutta 2010), 21.
23. Swapna Bhattacharya, "Some Observations on Mahayana–Tantric Beliefs in Ancient Myanmar," *Journal of the Department of Ancient Indian History and Culture* 20: 59.
24. Swapna Bhattacharya, "The Ari Cult of Myanmar," in *Tradition and Modernity in Myanmar*, U. Gaertner and J. Lorenz (eds.) (Muenster 1994), 251–71.
25. Sukumar Sen, *Buddhism in Southeast Asia* (Calcutta, n.d.). On Nagarjunkonda and its archaeological description see Sukumar Dutt, *Buddhist Monks and Monasteries in India* (Delhi: Motilal Banarasidass 1962), 126–37.
26. For Abeyadana and all temples of Pagan see Paul Strachan, *Pagan: Art & Architecture of old Burma* (Whiting Bay: Kiscadale Publication 1989).
27. Swapna Bhattacharya, "Religion and Colonial Politics: Assam, Myanmar," in *Development Dynamics in North East India*, Jayanta Kumar Ray and Rakhee Bhattacharya (eds.) (Delhi: Anshah Publishing House and Maulana Abul Kalam Azad Institute of Asian Studies, Kolkata 2008), 309–29.
28. Hirakawa Akira, *A History of Indian Buddhism: From Shakyamuni to early Mahayana* (Delhi: Motilal Banarasidass 2007).
29. Biswanath Banerjee discussed the social environment which opened the door for syncretic tradition in Buddhism. See Biswanath Banerjee, "Buddhism and Syncretism," *Journal of the Asiatic Society* 46, no. 1 (2004): 10.
30. Ananda Guruge (ed.), *Anagarika Dharmapal: Return to Righteousness* (Ministry of Cultural Affairs and Information, Ministry of Socio-cultural Integration, Department of Cultural Affairs, Sri Lanka 1991), 732.

31. Shanti Swarrop Bauddh, *Bodhgaya: The Great Sacred Place of Buddhists* (New Delhi: Samyak Prakashan 2008), 44–47.
32. Michael W. Charney, "Beyond State-centered Histories in Western Burma: Missionizing Monks and Intra-regional Migrants in the Arakan Littoral, c. 1784-1860," in *Maritime Frontier of Burma*, Jos Gommans and Jacques Leider (eds.) (Leiden: KITLV Press, n.d.), 221.
33. *Kusinagara*, Archaeological Survey of India, Government of India, New Delhi, 2006, 19.
34. Varasambodhi Thera, *Sachitra Bauddha Tirtha Parikrama* (Bodhgaya: International Meditation Centre 2007), 44.
35. Rana P. B Singh, *Where the Buddha Walked* (Banaras: Indica Books 2003), 158.
36. *The Life Story of Sri Bhaddanta Chandramani Mahathera*, U Sein Tun Aung (trans.) and Josephine Williams (ed.) (Sarnath: Chandramani Foundation, Burmese Buddhist Temple, n.d.), 21.
37. Swapna Bhattacharya, "Rabindranath Tagore in Myanmar (Burma) and Tagore's Perception of Southeast Asia India Relations," in *Interrogating History : Essays for Hermann Kulke*, Shishir K. Panda and Martin Brandtner (eds.) (Delhi: Monohar 2006), 212–29.
38. T.W. Rhys Davids, *Buddhist India* (Delhi: Low Price Publications, [1903] 2010), 40.
39. Sanjay Kumar, *Tha Vaishali* (Patna: Unique Computer & Screen Printers 2002), 11. See for all the Buddhist sites, D.C. Ahir, *Buddhist Sites and Shrines in India, History, Art and Architecture* (Delhi: Sree Satguru Publications 2003).
40. Rhys Davids, *Buddhist India*, 37.
41. Vesali is 9 km south of Dhanyavati. It was founded around the beginning of the sixth century and named after the Indian city of Vaisali/Vesali. See P. Gutman, *Burma's Lost Kingdom: Splendours of Arakan* (Bangkok: Orchid Press 2001), 10.
42. Dutt, *Buddhist Monks and Monasteries in India*, 58–65.
43. Bauddh, *Bodhgaya*, 45; on Burmese inscription at Bodhgaya see Taw Sein ko, *Burmese Sketches* (Rangoon: British Burma Press, n.d.), 90.

44. *Centennial Celebration of Dhammachakka Vihar Migadawon Myanmar Temple Souvenir Volume (1908-2008)*, Saranath, Varanasi, 2008, 55–61.
45. Ahir, *Buddhist Sites and Shrines in India*, 90ff.
46. Bhattacharya, *India and Myanmar*, 24–26.
47. Swapna Bhattacharya, "From Mahabodhi Movement of the late 19th century (1891) to Neo-Buddhist Revival (1956) in Post Colonial India," in *Myanmar Historical Commission. Conference Proceedings* (Golden Jubilee), Yangon 2005, 339–64. See also Swapna Bhattacharya, *India-Myanmar Relations 1886-1948* (Kolkata: K.P. Bagchi 2007).

6

Orthodox Christianity and Buddhism: From Confrontation to Cooperation?

Olga V. Buraeva

Orthodox Christianity began to spread among the Buryats systematically from the year 1681, from the base of the Daurian Mission. With a view to spread Christianity among the peoples of Eastern Siberia the Irkutsk eparchy was created in 1727. However, on the whole their success was poor. Since the seventeenth century Orthodoxy encountered Buddhism which had penetrated to the Trans-Baikal from Tibet and Mongolia, and turned out to be a serious rival in the struggle for human souls. Buddhism spread first among the Selenga Buryats, approximately in the seventeenth century, then among the Khori Buryats since the mid-seventeenth century, among the Alarsk and Tunkin Buryats in the nineteenth century while to the other genus of Buryats of Cis-Baikal

---

Original Paper in Russian: Pravoslavie i buddizm: ot protivostoyaniya k vzaimodeistviyu?—Translated by Susmita Bhattacharya.

Buddhism began to penetrate in the beginning of twentieth century.

Until the middle of the nineteenth century there was no single religious centre widely recognized by the Buryat tribes and clans; there was close contest between different tribal groups of *noyonstvo*[1] and the clergy of Selenga as well as Khori Buryats for dominant position in the administration by the Trans-Baikal Lamaist monasteries—the *datsans*. By adopting the "Regulations of the Lamaist clergy in Eastern Siberia of 1853," the Tsarist Government completed the process of consolidation of the Buddhist church. Buddhism became officially recognized religion of the Buryats and Lamaism received a number of privileges over the Orthodox missionaries.

These "Regulations" evoked extreme discontent of the Synod and the Orthodox Mission, which began to strive for changes in the Regulations, abolition of those privileges that were given to the Buddhist church. Activation of missionary struggle against Buddhism was associated with the reorganization of the missionary affairs. During the years 1865–68 the Orthodox Missionary Society was formed, which was to improve organizing the affairs in the remote border regions of Russia. In 1861, instead of Daurian was formed Transbaikalian. In 1882, Archbishop Veniamin was appointed as the chief of the Mission.

In the second half of the nineteenth century the activities of the missionaries intensified and several missionary camps were opened. By 1870 there were 22 camps as part of the Irkutsk and the Trans-Baikal Mission, in seven years it was

35, and in the beginning of the twentieth century the number went up to 41. However, the success of the Mission was insignificant. From1862 to 1890, about 200 people from the Shamanists were baptized by the Trans-Baikal Mission. Archbishop Veniamin explained such fallout by the adverse conditions created as a consequence of strengthening of Buddhism. Therefore, in the second half of the nineteenth century the activities of the mission mainly aimed at securing administrative restrictions of Buddhism.

The Mission demanded the cancellation of the "Regulations" of 1853, wiping out the rank and privileges of Hambo Lama, liquidating land holdings of the *datsans*, and prohibiting the Mongolian lamas from coming to Trans-Baikal. The Mission supported the acceleration of land and administrative reforms, believing that these measures would break the alliance between the *noyonstvo* and lamas, thereby weakening Buddhism and creating favourable conditions for the spread of Orthodoxy. In 1863, Archbishop Veniamin made an official note "On Lamaist idolatrous superstition in Eastern Siberia," in which he demanded considerable changes in the Regulations, abandonment of encouraging policy with regard to Buddhism and abolition of all privileges, etc.

In 1863, a special committee was formed at the headquarters of the Eastern Siberia to review the materials of Veniamin. However, the committee admitted that the "Regulations" of 1853 "is on the whole consistent with the outlook of the government." The mission was denied all its demands.

In 1866, Archbishop Veniamin appealed to the Synod. The Chief Procurator of the Synod through the Department of Religious Affairs of Foreign Faiths tried to achieve partial changes in the "Regulations." The Synod proposed to change the procedure of approval of Hambo Lama's position by Tsar's name, as this gave him an undeserved authority, and to hand over this function to the provincial authorities. The demand was placed to impose tariff on the collection for performing occasional religious rites and deny entry to the Mongolian and Tibetan lamas into Russia. The Ministry of Internal Affairs in response to all the demands of the Synod said that taking measures to restraint Lamaism was "contrary to the spirit of our legislation."

The Mission's demands were too blunt and did not take into account the political implications. Therefore, the provincial and central administration did not support the attempts of the Mission to crush Buddhism by means of direct police oppressions.

Not being able to weaken Buddhism, the Orthodox Mission raised a number of questions concerning the general conditions of its activities. The nomadic way of life and opposition of the alien authorities were referred to as the objective reasons that were hindering the spread of Orthodoxy. The Orthodox Mission saw the strength of Lamaism in nomadic cattle-breeding based economy as well as domestic, cultural and administrative isolation of the Buryat departments. Therefore, it set high hopes on the reforms in the administrative as well as land regulations of the Buryats and by all means pressed for their adoption. The Orthodox Mission believed that the curtailment of land holdings would compel the Buryats to move to agriculture and settled way of life, which in turn would level the features of day-to-day life style of the Buryats and merge them with the Russian population of the *krai*. The economic demolition of the nomadic way of life was to be done by administrative reform, by liquidating the steppe dumas and replacing them according to the model of Russian peasant administration. But the adoption of these reforms was postponed till a more favourable time.

In the conditions of reaction that set in after the liquidation of the revolutionary situation in the years 1879–80, when the militant autocracy, militant Orthodoxy and great-power chauvinism were proclaimed to be the foundation of the political system, the Orthodox Mission recommenced its demands, which found strong support in the Synod. In 1883, the Chief Procurator of the Synod Pobedonostsev accused the provincial government of inadequate monitoring of Lamaism and for being in connivance with the Lamaist clergy. As a result, an investigation started. But, despite the support of the Synod, this time also the matter pertaining to restriction of Buddhism could not be resolved immediately. The church reform was to be preceded by a reform in the social structure of the Buryats. Only the abolition of estates of the *noyons*' class as well as administrative privileges enjoyed by them and thereby depriving Buddhism of their support by taking the course of administrative power could weaken it. Thus, the reform in the administrative department of the Buryats was placed in view of the conditions of spreading Orthodoxy.

This question was raised in 1885 at the Congress of the Bishops in Irkutsk. The Congress designed the implementation of land and administrative reforms that were supposed to put an end to the nomadic way of life and bring the Buryat to forced settled way of life. Disputes and disagreements came up apropos of these reforms.

The Archbishop Veniamin continued to insist on changing the "Regulations" of 1853. At the request of Pobedonostsev Alexander III accepted it. As a result of the efforts of the Synod and the Mission, in 1886 the Department of Religious Affairs began to prepare a meeting on the matter of lamas.

In 1892, a meeting on the matter of the lamas was held in St. Petersburg, which was attended by Pobedonostsev and the representatives of the ministries of foreign affairs, internal affairs and public properties. The meeting admitted that the position of the Lamaist clergy should be restructured because it was not satisfactory and hindering the activities of the Orthodox mission. It was decided to improve the composition of the mission, equip the churches with modern facilities and amend some church rites. The Ministry of Internal Affairs was instructed to prepare a new draft of the "Regulations." The Orthodox mission strived in such a way that the question of Lamaism was resolved by taking into account its interests.

In 1877, the Trans-Baikal Spiritual Mission had 18 camps with 17 missionaries and 17 junior deacons. At the same time, within the system Buddhist church there were 34 datsans, and Hambo Lama in them, 34 *shiretuis*,[2] 216 *lama-gelungs*,[3] 34 *bandis*[4] and *khuvaraks*[5] — altogether 285 authorized lamas, but in reality it was much higher.

For justice' sake, it is worth mentioning that although the Buddhist priests did not oppose the Orthodox Church, but they vigorously campaigned against the entire Russian as well as Western farming and settled way of life, against European culture and education, while disseminating their teachings and moral directives as well as the Mongolian and Tibetan traditions in the social and family life, moulding the way of life necessary for themselves and the morals of the believers.

In the endeavour to attract the Buryats to their faith the Orthodox lost to Buddhism. Success was probably due to the fact that the Buddhist preachers could better understand the queries of the local people. In addition, the lamas addressed them in their native language. They taught people to read and write Mongolian and medically treated them. The strengths of the Orthodox missionaries and Buddhist clergy were unequal. In their reports the missionaries noted with bitterness the inability to resist the army of lamas who were more close to the life of the Buryats.

The Missionaries' Congress held in1908 stated that promoting Buddhism not only among the non-Russian but also the Russian population was a problem of the near future. In the years of Revolution of 1905 and especially after the appearance of the Decree of 17 October 1905, according to which the people of the Russian empire were granted religious freedom, the mass desertion from the Orthodoxy began. Thus, if there were about 10 thousand baptized Buryats in Tunkinsk Mission, after the decree almost all of them converted to Buddhism. During this period, the Buddhist clergy invigorated their activities on the west side of Lake Baikal: *datsans* and other buildings of religious worship were opened. Everywhere the conflicts on religious ground were settled.

During the period from 1905 to 1917, however, the number

of new parishes and churches in Siberia as a whole also had a growing trend (due to mass resettlements and growth of population in Siberia during the period of Stolypin reforms).

Nevertheless, there was marked dialogue between Buddhism and Orthodox Christianity and prospects appeared to be good. On 28 January 1912 Irkutsk was visited by the head of the Buddhist church Pandido Hambo Lama Itigelov, a progressive man, interested in anything that might elevate the Buryat culture.

However, after 1917 the Orthodox Christianity and Buddhism were subject to persecution, as a result of the repressive and radical policy of Bolshevism. After the appearance of the Decree on the Separation of Church from the State, and of School from church in 1918, a fight with religion developed. In the territory of Buryatiya it started from 1925, when the churches were defiled and desecrated, the church valuables were confiscated, many priests were subject to repression and a part of them were shot dead. By 1932, 272 Orthodox, 43 Buddhist, 81 Old Believers, 4 Jewish, 5 Mohammedan, 4 Evangelical Christian, that is, altogether 409 associations were functioning in Buryatiya. By the end of '30s not a single functioning temple remained in Buryatiya.

During the years of Great Patriotic War, revival of religiosity of the population was observed. On 4 May 1945 the Orthodox parish of the Holy Voznesenskaya Church was opened in Ulan-Ude and sometime later the parish of the Uspenskaya Church in Kyakhta, which was shut down in 1962. These were the only ones in the whole republic.

In 1990 the "Law on Freedom of Religion" was adopted,

and in April 1994, by decision of the Holy Synod of the ROC[6] the Dioceses of Chita and Trans-Baikal were established, being separated from that of the Irkutsk and Chita. In March 1994, by the decree of His Grace, Vadim (Lazebnii), the Bishop of Irkutsk and Chita, the Buryat Deanery was formed within the Republic of Buryatiya. On 1 January 1994, 7 Orthodox and 3 Buddhist societies were registered in the republic, and in 2000, the number of the Orthodox was already 56, while the Buddhist ones-37. At present, 71 Orthodox parishes, 50 Buddhist societies and 38 *datsans* are functioning in Buryatiya.

Once the Dalai Lama XIV spoke in connection with mutual relations of religious dogmas. He said that for the followers of different religious systems to be able to achieve harmony, they should have the opportunity to know and understand each other. I think that the representatives of Orthodox Christianity and Buddhism are well aware of this. During the ceremonial events (laying of the foundation-stone, sending-off colleague police officers to serve in the Caucasus, etc.) in which there is a gathering of Buddhist and Orthodox laymen, the rites of consecration are performed by both the priests and lamas, showing thereby respect to each other. The representatives of different religions set the laymen on the right path, inculcate into their consciousness the good moral principles of different faiths by finding common values, they save the souls of the believers, help the orphans, lonely people, the sufferers, the sick as well as mourning persons and besides, in their sermons of religious doctrines they do not insult each other, and thus laying the foundation of mutual relations between all the confessions. And in the hearts of people, these religions have found understanding for a long time. According to our research, 55 per cent of the Russians and Buryats believe that God is one, only the roads to Him are different. Furthermore, one of the characteristics of the population of modern Buryatiya is a syncretism of religious beliefs.

Notes and References

Translator's Note

1. *Noyonstvo*: a. The class of rich herd-owners of the eastern Buryatiya. b. A clan aristocracy called in Mongolian *noyons*.
2. *Shiretui:* Chief Lama.
3. *Gelung*: the third monastic rank in Lamaism, who has adopted 253 vows.
4. *Bandi:* the lowest monastic rank in Lamaism, a novice, who has taken five vows.
5. *Khuvarak:* a student monk.
6. Russian Orthodox Church.

For further reading please see

Aziatskaya Rossiya, Lyudi i Poryadki Uralom (St. Petersburg 1914), T.1.

M.N. Bogdanov, *Ocherki istorii buryat-mongol'skogo naroda* (Verkhneudinsk: Burmongiz 1926), 230.

O.V. Buraeva, *Khozyaistvennye i etnokul'turnye svyazi russkikh, buryat i evenkov v XVII - seredine XIX v.* (Ulan-Ude: Izd-vo BNC SB RAS 2000), 206.

Buryatskie letopisi (Ulan-Ude 1995), 198.

A.D. Zhalsaraev, *Poseleniya, pravoslavnye khramy, svyaschennosluzhiteli Buryatii XVII-XX stoletii* (Ulan-Ude: Buryat kn. Izd-vo 2001), 447.

Zakon Respubliki Buryatiya "O religioznoi deyatel'nosti na territorii

Respubliki Buryatiya" ot 23dekabrya 1997g, in *Iz istorii religioznykh konfessii Buryatii XX vek. Sb. Dokumentov* (Ulan-Ude 2001), 238–44.

P. Kropotkin, *Poezdka v Okinskii karaul*, Zap. SO RGO Irkutsk, 1867, Kn. IX, X, 1–95.

F.A. Kudryatsev, *Istoriya Buryat-mongol'skogo naroda s XVII v. do 60-kh godov XIX v.* M.; L.: AN SSSR (1940): 242.

I.M. Manzhigeev, *Yangutskii buryatskii rod (opyt istoriko-etnograficheskogo issledovaniya)* (Ulan-Ude 1960), 232.

T.M. Mikhailov, "Vliyanie lamaizma i khristianstva na shamanism Buryat," in *Khristianstvo i lamaizm u korennogo naseleniya Sibiri* (L.: Nauka 1979), 127–49.

T.M. Mikhailov, *Istoriya i kul'tura buryatskogo naroda* (Ulan-Ude: Belig 1999), 248.

V.T. Mikhailova, *Pravoslavie v dukhovnoi kul'ture buryat* (*30-e gg. XVIIv. – 1917 g.*) (Ulan-Ude: Izd-vo BSGTU 1999), 174.

Novyi entsiklopedicheskii slovar', SPb.: Izd-vo Brokgauza F.A. i Efrona I. A., T. 25, 324–25.

Ocherki istorii kul'tury Buryatii (Ulan-Ude 1972), 490.

I.A. Podgorbunskii, *Buryaty (fizicheskii tip i dukhovnaya lichnost' buryat)* (Irkutsk 1903), 32.

Pribavleniya k "Irkutskim epakhal'nym vedomstvam," no. 18 (1887).

Pribavleniya k "Irkutskim epakhal'nym vedomstvam," no. 4 (1888).

N.S. Romanov, *Letopis' goroda Irkutska* (Irkutsk 1994), chapter 3.

Sbornik dokumentov po istorii Buryatii, XVII vek. (Ulan-Ude 1960), Vyp., 1, 493 c.

Svedeniya o religioznykh ob'edineniyakh, proshedshikh pereregistratsiyu v Ministerstve yustitsii Respubliki Buryatiya po sostoyaniyu na 9 avgusta 2000 g., in *Iz istorii religioznykh konfessii Buryatii XX vek. Sb. Dokumentov* (Ulan-Ude 2001), 249–56.

I.I. Serebrennikov, *Inorodtsy Vostochnoi Sibiri, ikh sostav i zanyatiya (Stat. ocherk)* (Irkutsk 1913), 48.

P.A. Slovtsov, *Istoricheskoe obozrenie Sibiri,* V 2 kn. SPb., 1886. Kn. 2, S 1772 po 1823 god.

Trudy pravoslavnykh missii Irkutskoi eparkhii, T. III, Irkutsk, 1885.
"Tserkov' i rusifikatsiya buryat-mongol pri tsarizme," *Krasnyi Arkhiv* (1932), T. 4 (53).
Yu. P. Shagdurov, "Gosudarstvo i religioznye konfessii Buryatii v 20-30-kh gg.," in *Issledovaniya po istorii Sibiri, Tsentral'noi i Vostochnoi Azii*, Ulan-Ude: Izd-vo Buryat gos. un-ta, 1998, 65-82.
M.M. Shmulevich, *Troitsko-Selenginskii monastyr'* (Ulan-Ude: Buryat. kn. izd-vo 1982), 64.

List of Contributors

Baatr U. Kitinov, Associate Professor, Department of the World History, Peoples' Friendship University of Russia, Moscow.

Rashmi Doraiswamy, Professor, Academy of International Studies, Jamia Millia Islamia New Delhi.

Manju Kak, Independent writer and scholar, earlier Visiting Professor with Jamia Millia Islamia and currently editor of a volume on Nicholas Roerich.

Tsymzhit P. Vanchikova, Professor, Head of the Centre of Oriental Manuscripts and Xylographs of the Institute of Mongolian, Buddhist and Tibetan Studies of the Siberian Branch of the Russian Academy of Sciences, Ulan Ude.

Swapna Bhattacharya (Chakraborti), Professor, Department of South & Southeast Asian Studies, University of Calcutta.

Olga V. Buraeva, Research Fellow and Head of the Ethnology group, Department of History, Ethnology and Sociology, Institute Mongolian, Buddhist and Tibetan Studies, SB RAS, Ulan Ude.

Index